All The best!

Liam

THE REVISED AND EXPANDED
SLEDGER'S HANDBOOK

HOW TO DELIVER THE PERFECT
CRICKETING INSULT

Liam McCann

THE REVISED AND EXPANDED
SLEDGER'S HANDBOOK
HOW TO DELIVER THE PERFECT
CRICKETING INSULT
by Liam McCann

Published by
Facts, Figures & Fun, an imprint of AAPPL
Artists' and Photographers' Press Ltd.
Church Farm House, Wisley, Surrey, GU23 6QL
info@aappl.com   www.aappl.com

Sales and Distribution
UK and export: Turnaround Publisher Services Ltd.
orders@turnaround-uk.com
Australia & New Zealand: Peribo Pty
michael.coffey@peribo.com.au

ISBN   9781904332589

Design (contents) Stefan Nekuda office@nekuda.at
Design (cover) Malcolm Couch malfolio@sky.com
Printed in China by: Imago Publishing info@imago.co.uk

CONTENTS

*This book is dedicated to Fiona Delevingne, the
sweariest person I know.*

1
WHAT DOES SLEDGING MEAN?

Sledging is the art of verbally intimidating a batsman so that he loses his concentration and gets himself out. It is also known as the art of initiating mental disintegration. The fielding side may use a variety of tactics to do this, including: the witty welcome, where the fielders try to upset the incoming batsman immediately; the chirp, where a fielder (usually the wicketkeeper) tries to engage the batsman in a battle of wits to divert his attention from the game; the behind the back shout, where any one of the fielders may suggest a new tactic to remove the batsman; the unexpected question, which may be so shocking and have nothing at all to do with cricket that the batsman loses concentration; the observation, which usually relates to the batsman's technique; the aggressive rant, where the bowler deliberately appears to get wound up; the sarcastic dig, where the bowler taunts the batsman; and the send off, where, having got out, the batsman is sent on his way with a volley of abuse ringing in his ears. The word itself appears to derive from the observation that New South Wales cricketer Grahame Corling was as subtle as a sledgehammer having sworn and offended his host at a party, although an alternative explanation has Corling's wife having an affair with a team-mate.

When Corling came in to bat in his next match, opposing players started singing the Percy Sledge song *When a Man loves a Woman.*

ORIGINS

It is commonly believed that the Australian sides of the 1960s and '70s started these dirty tactics (which are considered gamesmanship now), but the father of rule bending was, in fact, the champion of English cricket at the end of the nineteenth century, Doctor William Gilbert Grace, known affectionately as WG. There are numerous stories about the great man using all kinds of tactics to unsettle his opponents. In one match he pointed out a flock of birds as they flew in front of the sun. Sensing that the batsman had been dazzled by the sunshine, Grace sent down one of his quicker balls and clean bowled him. In another instance he was bowled himself first ball. The mood of the crowd changed as most had been forced to pay a sixpence entry fee instead of the usual three just because WG was playing. The doctor didn't disappoint, however. He simply replaced the bails and chastised the bowler with:

"They've come to see me bat, young man, not to watch you bowl."

He was also well known for replacing the bails if the slightest touch of the ball had dislodged them (which he believed the umpire wouldn't have been able to hear), and then remarking on the strength of the wind, as if that had been the cause of his downfall. On hearing this excuse, one umpire gave him his marching orders with:

"Let us hope that wind helps the good doctor on his journey back to the pavilion."

It is said that Grace once skied a ball, watched two fielders head towards each other to make the catch, and then, as they were about to collide, shouted "Mine". Both men stopped running, the ball fell to the ground, and Grace made the single. (This tactic was resurrected in an Abinger Hammer versus Surrey Celebrities fixture by an unnamed player in the 1980s. It was still frowned upon then, one hundred years after Grace had used it.)

Historians agree that WG would bully umpires into giving him favourable decisions, that he told Australian ground-staff how to prepare their pitches to suit him when on tour there, and that he verbally intimidated opponents as the first of the 'sledgers'.

Grace was not above resorting to more desperate measures if he felt the opposing batsmen were taking the game away from his side. On one occasion he concealed the ball in his beard, waited for one of the batsmen to leave his ground to prod a bump in the pitch, and then flicked off the bails and appealed to the umpire for the run out. He would even ply his crafty trade in the outfield, a place he rarely ventured as he aged (claiming that the ground was getting too far away to reach), often pretending to miss-field the ball. More often than not, the batsmen would try and take a sneaky single but as soon as they were halfway down the pitch WG would produce the ball and rifle it in to the 'keeper for the run out. Although this practice was rarely used in the Test match arena thereafter, Trevor Bailey reintroduced it in the 1950s. Bailey was so noted for his slow play that he once elicited this remark from South African pace bowler Peter Heine:

"I want to hit you, Bailey. I want to hit you over the heart."

Chris Tavaré was also a master at grinding out an innings, prompting one observer to comment:

"Watching Tavaré was a bit like waiting to die."

While another commentator, after the batsman had taken seven hours to score 78 in the second innings, backing up his five-hour 69 in the first, said:

"Only Tavaré could make a 69 boring."

But let's get back to Grace for a moment. This next quote was rearranged by Fred Trueman in similar circumstances more than half a century later. Essex bowler Charles Kortwright had watched the umpire turn down a plumb LBW shout as well as a blatant caught behind off a big nick before he uprooted two of Grace's stumps with his next delivery. He waited for Grace to turn towards the pavilion before remarking:

"Surely you're not walking, Doctor? Why, there's one stump still standing."

In June 1878 Grace's Australian friend and star player Billy Midwinter was at Lord's for his country's match against Middlesex, while his county (Gloucestershire) was on its way to The Oval to play Surrey. The Gloucestershire team somehow managed to turn up a man short so a couple of players, led by WG, headed over to Lord's to persuade Midwinter to make up the numbers. As they left Lord's, three of the Australian players gave chase and an angry altercation followed. Grace was fuming and in front of several bystanders was heard to bellow:

"You Australians are a damned lot of sneaks!"

He apologised later but still got his way. Midwinter played for Gloucestershire for the rest of the season, although he wasn't allowed to play against the tourists. The Australian newspapers reacted with:

"We in Australia do not take kindly to WG. For such a big man he is surprisingly tenacious on very small points."

This turned out to be a controversial season for Grace. In a match against Surrey at Clifton he played the ball but it looped up and caught in the folds of his shirt. He, naturally, started running and had completed several before the fielding side forced him to stop. Grace, of course, had an answer for everything:

"If I'd given it back, you'd have claimed I'd handled the ball."

As usual, he got his way and was awarded three runs. Sadly, stories about the great man were not always so humorous or sporting. In a Test match against the Australians at The Oval in 1882, batsman Sam Jones played the ball to Grace who was fielding close in. Jones knew a run was not on so stayed his ground. Grace then cheekily beckoned him over and threw down the stumps as soon as he was out of his crease. Fred Spofforth was so incensed by the wicket that he demolished England the following day with figures of seven for 44. It was then that the mock obituary for English cricket appeared in *The Sporting Times* and the legend of the Ashes was born.

*

Although sledging was not considered gentlemanly at the time and seemed, temporarily perhaps, to die out after WG's retirement from first class cricket in 1908, there had always been an undercurrent of hostility between the English and Australian players. Lord Harris's 1878-79 tour to Australia set the trend for many of the ill-tempered Ashes clashes to follow, although the urn itself was not at stake. The home side hammered the English in the first Test in Melbourne, with the tourists' captain so disappointed in his own performance that he hurled his bat across the pavilion. The bad feelings rolled over to the Sydney Test, and when Australian umpire George Coulthard adjudged local hero Billy Murdoch run out, two thousand spectators invaded the pitch and began attacking the English players. Lord Harris was beaten with a whip, Albert Hornby had his shirt ripped off and six English players were forced to defend themselves with stumps. In retaliation, many English clubs refused to play the touring Australians when they visited the following year.

*

In 1884 umpire George Hodges refused to appear on the pitch on day three of the fifth Test because he was so upset at the amount of abuse hurled at him by England's fielders. Earlier in the series Australia had taken the field with only nine players because the rest felt that the English team were being paid too much. While trying to resolve the argument Billy Barnes broke his hand on a wall after missing Australian skipper Percy McDonnell with a punch. Surprisingly, given these outbursts, there followed a few years of relative harmony – WG's antics notwithstanding – until the most controversial series in history.

*

The 'Bodyline' tour of 1932-33 simply highlighted the fact that the teams would try anything to emerge victorious in a series, particularly when the Ashes were at stake. The tour brought home the dangers of fast, short-pitched bowling to unprotected batsman, and also provoked massive slanging matches between the two countries in the media, with the Australians furious about the leg theory tactic as it nullified their star batsman, Donald Bradman. The media war of words soon filtered onto the pitch, something of a foregone conclusion given the rivalry between the two sides. England's Bill Voce was heard to warn Vic Richardson:

"If we don't beat you, we'll knock your bloody heads off."

Australian captain Bill Woodfull replied, summing up the thoughts of a nation with:

"There are two teams out there. One of them is attempting to play cricket and the other is not."

England captain Douglas Jardine decided to take things a step further with:

"All Australians are an uneducated and unruly mob."

Now it's one thing to sledge an opponent, but Jardine, an upper-class English gent, was sticking it to the entire country and his popularity took a nosedive. He didn't seem to mind:

"I've not travelled ten thousand miles to make friends. I'm here to win the Ashes."

Ian Botham also received a bit of rough treatment in the 1980s when he returned home from a tour of Pakistan and joked:

"Pakistan is the sort of country you send your mother-in-law on an all-expenses holiday to."

Pakistan's Aamer Sohail was none too pleased about this, but he exacted revenge when they beat England in the 1992 World Cup Final. He confronted Botham with:

"Why don't you send your mother-in-law out to play? She can't do much worse."

Botham briefly played professional football for Scunthorpe United. If he was having a bad day with bat or ball, it was not uncommon for opposing players to remind him of those early days:

"You should have stuck to soccer."

Harold Larwood could be equally disparaging about the all-rounder:

"He's the most overrated player I've ever seen. He's too heavy and his bowling wouldn't burst a paper bag."

But let's get back to 'Bodyline' briefly. Jardine refused to buckle to the media pressure and let his fast bowlers do their talking on the pitch. Woodfull was felled by a sickening Larwood bouncer to the chest (to cries of

"Well bowled, Harold!"), wicketkeeper Bert Oldfield wound up in hospital with a fractured skull and Stan McCabe had to plead with his mother not to attack the bowlers should he be injured. The Australian Cricket Board finally decided to intervene, sending this telegram to the MCC:

"Bodyline bowling is causing intensely bitter feelings between our players as well as injury. In our opinion it is unsportsmanlike. Unless stopped at once, it is likely to upset the friendly relations between England and Australia."

England refused to back down and went on to take the series 4-1, but they won few fans with their hostile bowling and un-gentlemanly conduct. Larwood recalls the aftermath:

"A cricket tour in Australia would be a delightful period in one's life, if one was deaf."

The tactic was rarely used thereafter, the players perhaps hoping to retrieve the lost spirit of the game.

*

England were not good enough to trouble the 1948 'Invincibles' either on or off the pitch, the incomparable Bradman in the twilight of his career still proving too strong. The great England opener, Jack Hobbs, fired a complimentary insult in Bradman's direction as a result:

"You're too good. You're spoiling the game."

But by 1958-59 England arrived in Australia with their best chance of returning home with the urn. Jim Laker summed up the mood in the camp with:

"The main aim of English cricket is, in fact, to beat Australia."

England captain Peter May recalls watching Aussie pace-man Ian Meckiff bowl in the tour match against Victoria before the first Test:

"He was throwing the ball at a batsman. This seemed an odd way for a bowler to limber up, but a few minutes later he was out in the middle bowling to Peter Richardson with exactly the same action."

The Australians countered that Meckiff was prevented from straightening his arm completely – and thus bowled with a bent arm action – due to a genetic abnormality, and his bowling helped defeat the tourists 4-0. This problem with straightening the bowling arm has also affected Muttiah Muralitharan, the Sri Lankan off-spinner. Murali suffered hugely at the hands of the Australian crowds whenever he toured there. He was no-balled by umpire Darrell Hair for 'chucking' in the Boxing Day Test in Melbourne in 1995 and promptly refused to tour the country. Hair has said that he'll no-ball the spinner again, calling his action:

"Diabolical."

In the spinner's defence, he was fitted with a brace that locked his arm as straight as possible and he still managed to bowl the infamous 'doosra'. Laws were then introduced to allow a degree of flex at the elbow and Murali continued tormenting batsmen with his devilish off-spin. But, according to Wisden (Source: *Cricketers' Almanack 2004*), that didn't stop England captain Nasser Hussain allegedly welcoming him to the crease in Kandy in 2003 with:

"He's an effing cheat and an effing chucker."

It can be equally effective to use the psychological sledge:

"You'd say that Boy George was straight."

✳

Fast bowler John Snow was included in Ray Illingworth's side that toured Australia in 1970-71. He was determined to unsettle the home team with his fiery temper and hostile bowling and, in the final Test at the Sydney Cricket Ground, he made the impact many had hoped to avoid. Having subjected the middle order to his full arsenal of ribcage-length balls, he bounced Terry Jenner, the ball striking the tail-ender on the head. The crowd was incensed, and Snow was roundly booed as he returned to field on the boundary at the end of the over.

Unrepentant, he was then peppered with beer cans and assaulted by the drunk who appeared to have consumed most of them.

Illingworth tried to restore order by approaching the crowd and pleading for calm but he was eventually forced to lead his team from the field. They only reappeared when the match referee warned them that they would forfeit the match if they refused to play on. Snow went on to take 31 wickets in the series and England retuned home triumphant (2-0). Ted Dexter summed up the tourists' view of the experience with:

"I have, on occasion, taken a reasonable dislike to Australians."

Four years later the ruthless team that took England on was labelled 'The Ugly Australians', not, as you might think, because of the way they looked, but because of their hard-nosed cricket, uncompromising hostility and extreme verbal abuse. Former England batsman Tom Graveney said of their behaviour:

"It's an open secret that Ian Chappell and Rod Marsh used to encourage their players to give opposing batsmen a lot of verbal abuse to try to break their concentration. They used to vie with each other in profanity."

*

It wasn't long before England were under the cosh again

in Ashes contests, however. Jeff Thomson and Dennis Lillee, two of the greatest fast bowlers of all-time, tore through England's batting line-ups throughout the '70s, although Lillee's most controversial moment involved his batting. In December 1979 he walked out to the middle in Perth with an aluminium bat, designed and built by his friend Graham Monoghan. It was within the rules to brandish such a weapon but every time he struck the ball the noise echoed round the WACA like a broken church bell. Of course the English fielders got stuck in immediately but when their ears started ringing captain Mike Brearley objected to Lillee using the bat. The umpires agreed and Lillee was forced to swap to the more traditional willow, not before he'd hurled the metal bat across the pitch in a fit of petulance. But both he and Thomson were masters of intimidation with the ball in hand and liked to have a word with the batsmen in the middle. And by way of a warm up, they'd fire a broadside in the press before the match. Lillee first:

"I try to hit a batsman in the ribcage when I bowl a purposeful bouncer, and I want it to hurt so much that he doesn't want to face me any more."

"I really am trying to scare him and hurt him so that he at least knows I'm around."

And Thomson:

"I enjoy hitting a batsman more than taking him out. It doesn't worry me in the least to see a batsman hurt,

rolling around screaming and blood on the pitch."

"The sound of the ball hitting the batsman's skull was music to my ears."

"I can't wait to have a crack at England. Stuff that stiff upper lip crap. Let's see how stiff it is when it's split."

England's David 'Bumble' Lloyd felt the full force of Thomson's bowling in the Ashes series of 1974. At a team meeting before the game he'd boasted:

"I could play Thomson with my dick."

Sadly for Lloyd, he then went out and proved it. The boxes in those days didn't offer much protection (he said they could also have been used as soap holders) and when the ball struck it turned the box inside out:

"Everything that should have been in the box was forced through the holes and was now on the outside. I needed a welder to separate the remains of the box from its contents."

Having watched Lloyd double over and collapse in agony, and with the comment from the team meeting having been leaked, Thomson marched down the wicket and said:

"Now you can't."

When he was finally helped to his feet, Lloyd had no option but to retire hurt. The *Sydney Telegraph* was quick to jump on the hapless English:

"Ashes to ashes, dust to dust, if Thommo doesn't get you Lillee must."

Sussex batsman John Barclay was hit on the head by a Thomson bouncer in a warm-up game before the 1985 Ashes, so he turned to the umpire and asked:

"Is this a time for heroics or should I go off?"

Thomson was quick to reply with:

"I'd fuck off if I was you."

Another Australian fast bowler, Geoff Lawson, was also an expert in dishing out the Ashes abuse:

"There's nothing like the sound of flesh on leather to start the match."

England's Brian Close, often on the receiving end of some fearsome bowling, particularly against Australia and the West Indies, had an opinion on this hostility (taken from *Cassell's Sports Quotations*):

"Fast bowlers are bully boys. They dish it out but they can't take it."

This was nicely illustrated when Dennis Lillee repeatedly bounced Gary Sobers. He eventually got his man but as Sobers was on his way back to the pavilion he winked at Lillee and said:

"Just remember, Dennis, I can bowl a mean bouncer too. And I'm a much better batsman than you."

Of course he could have replied with a standard line:

"The thicker you are, the better your chances of becoming a fast bowler."

England's Tony Greig decided the best way to deal with Lillee was to fight fire with fire. He hurled down a couple of bouncers, one of which hit Lillee in the ribs, prompting Keith Fletcher to chirp:

"Well done, Tony. Give him another one."

So Greig bounced him again and Lillee, trying to hook the ball off his eyebrows, got a top edge and was caught. As he trudged back to the pavilion, Lillee looked across and frowned:

"Don't forget who started this, you lanky streak of piss. It's your turn next."

The great fast bowler was true to his word. He walked Fletcher all the way to the crease the following day, chatting to him while he took guard, and then peppering him with a barrage of short balls. When the initial confrontation was leaked to the press and they were asking questions about Tony Greig's motivation for firing Lillee up, he was quick to deny his comments had made any difference:

"Are you seriously saying that if I hadn't bounced Lillee, he'd have ambled in and bowled us half-volleys all day? That's absolute nonsense. He'd have been aiming at our bodies from ball one anyway."

*

The on-pitch Ashes exchanges in the early '80s went England's way, with both teams happy to share a beer and chew over the action after the day's play. Although the sledging continued it was mostly good-natured. When Tony Greig sledged Dennis Lillee for bowling too many slower balls, for example, Lillee replied with a ferocious bouncer that struck Greig on the helmet. When Greig took the helmet off to inspect it, wicketkeeper Rod Marsh quipped:

"Don't worry, I know a good panel beater."

Things changed when Allan Border took over the Australian captaincy for the 1984-85 series after previous captain Kim Hughes had broken down in tears at a press conference. He was determined not to suffer any more humiliating defeats at the hands of the old enemy (such as at Headingley in 1981, where England fought back to win having followed on with bookmakers offering odds of 500-1 against the possibility) and his sides toughened up mentally and physically. The upshot was that England were denied the Ashes for eighteen years. Border was so ruthless that he was once heard to sledge team-mate Dean Jones when they were touring the sub-continent. Jones had been suffering from the notorious Delhi Belly while in Madras during the tied Test in 1986-87, and he was struggling to contain emissions at both ends. After vomiting and suffering a particularly bad bout of cramp he asked Border if he could retire hurt, but Border was having none of it. He told Jones (a Victorian), depending on which quote you'd like to believe:

"Fine. Let's get a real Australian out here – a Queenslander."

"Stay out here or you'll never play for Australia again."

Jones did as his captain asked and went on to score a memorable 160 not out. It was this backbone that helped Border's sides demolish all-comers and set the tone for his country's dominance in international cricket for the next generation. And his wrath could also be directed at opposition players, this being saved for Robin Smith when the Englishman asked for a drink to be brought on:

"What do you think this is, a fucking tea party? No you can't have a fucking glass of water. You can fucking wait

like the rest of us."

And this line was delivered to England's Angus Fraser after the bowler had sledged Border for playing and missing:

"I've faced bigger, uglier bowlers than you, mate. Now fuck off and bowl the next one."

Fraser apparently huffed and puffed his way through a couple more overs before having a second bite at the Australian captain after he'd missed another ball:

"Why didn't you hit that one?"

Border had clearly been waiting for the line:

"Because I can't tell the difference between the ball and your face."

Fraser's plodding cart-horse-style run up also attracted attention:

"Are your braces caught in the sight-screen, Eeyore?"

Border must have been surprised to get a reply (of sorts) when, in their 1994 clash with South Africa, he said to Brian McMillan:

"For a big bloke you don't bowl very fast."

The South African's reply was non-verbal but intimidating

nonetheless. He is said to have entered the Australian dressing room at lunch and urged Border to repeat the sledge while pointing a pistol at his head!

England's players in particular were singled out for abuse by Border's teams throughout their period of dominance in the late '80s and '90s. With a typically boorish backhanded compliment Graham Hick was known to the Aussies as:

"Braveheart."

And to the Kiwis as:

"A flat-track bully."

He was usually greeted at the wicket by Merv Hughes with:

"So, Graham, what does your husband do while you're playing cricket?"

After a particularly brutal over consisting of two bouncers and four balls in the ribs, with each delivery punctuated by a prolonged bout of sledging, umpire Dickie Bird stepped in to restore order:

"Merv, what has poor Graham ever done to you?"

"He offended me in a previous life."

Hughes had clearly run out of usable lines and reverted to type when Robin Smith came in next:

"Does your husband play cricket as well?"

These lines are interchangeable with the equally overused:

"Does your boyfriend know you're here?"

"You'd better ring your mummy to tell her you'll be home by tea."

Hughes, a man said to have descended directly from a walrus, was a truly supreme sledger, although his vocabulary often failed to exceed the five standard words:

"Eff. Off. You. Pommie. Bastard."

He was also renowned for shouting at the batsman every time he missed the ball:

"Turn the bat over, mate. The instructions are on the other side."

Smith and Hughes were particularly fond of trading insults. Having played and missed at Hughes during the Lord's Test in 1989 the bowler steamed up to Smith and shouted:

"You can't fucking bat."

Robin Smith replied in the best way possible, by cracking Hughes's next delivery to the boundary. Then he said, adding insult to the four runs:

"Hey, Merv, we make a fine pair. I can't fucking bat and you can't fucking bowl!"

New Zealand's Mark Greatbatch recalls being stared down by the intimidating Victorian:

"He was so close I could smell his dodgy breath."

Michael Atherton was dismissed nineteen times in Tests by Glenn McGrath but it was big Merv who treated him to the most vigorous sledging assault. Atherton recalls (from his autobiography):

"Hughes was all bristle and bullshit and I couldn't make out what he was saying, except that every sledge ended with arsewipe."

Here's another classic from the Victorian:

"I'll bowl you a fucking piano, you Pommie poof; let's see if you can play that."

Atherton didn't really mind Hughes's sledging because some of his lines were so funny, but he did object to Steve Waugh's constant banter:

"He was the only one who got up my nose because he was always dishing out the verbals, which was a bit of a joke really as he was wetting himself against the quicker bowlers."

England were so outclassed by the Australians in the sledging stakes that by the end of the disastrous 1990-91 series, Graham Gooch summed up the thoughts of both team and nation with:

"We were like a fart competing with thunder."

England's pace bowler Gladstone Small, known to the Aussies – players and crowds alike – as 'Pearl' because he appeared to have no neck, commented in the *Observer Sport Monthly* in 2005 that Hughes:

"Would sledge his own mother if he thought it would help the cause."

He came pretty close while playing fellow countryman Jamie Brayshaw in a Victoria-South Australia clash with:

"You're a faggot, a cock-sucker, a dirty little prick."

Of course Small can be sledged with the simple but effective line:

"Do you have a more talented brother called Disraeli Big?"

*

English supporters gained their revenge for the John Snow incident in 2002-03. Aussie pace-man Brett Lee's action was under investigation by officials because some believed his arm was slightly bent at the time of delivery. (It has since been bio-medically proved with the help of super slow-motion cameras that most bowlers have some flex in their arm during delivery. The rules have now been changed so that all bowlers may have up to fifteen degrees of flex at the elbow. This is adjudged to be the point where the action becomes noticeably suspect to the umpire, although how they can decide between fourteen and sixteen degrees in the heat of a Test match battle is anyone's guess.) The English crowd had already made up their minds about Lee's action and repeatedly 'no-balled' him from the stands. They, of course, believed it was just a bit of harmless fun, the crowd sledging the players, but Justin Langer called it:

"An absolute disgrace."

How Langer responded when the shoe was on the other foot is not recorded. England's Simon Jones was tipped to be a major bowling force in that series but he suffered a horrific knee injury while fielding on the boundary at the Gabba, Brisbane. While he was lying on the ground in agony he could hear a voice in the crowd shouting at him. At first he couldn't hear exactly what was being said but it soon became clear:

"Get up, you weak Pommie bastard!"

Proof that sledging is never confined to just the players and the media. Another fan started throwing cans at the helpless Englishman, actions that so incensed Steve Harmison that he said:

"I felt like jumping the fence and doing a 'Cantona'."

*

As the 2005 series approached, and many thought that England had their best chance of regaining the urn since the days of Botham, Gatting and Gower, the media war warmed up nicely. Players from both teams were writing newspaper columns, so the long-distance sledging began as far back as July 2004. Steve Harmison promised to:

"Batter the Aussies."

The ever-confident Glenn McGrath replied with this customary score prediction:

"We'll win the series 5-0. I'd be letting myself and my team-mates down if I said anything else. If a couple of matches are affected by the rain, we'll still win 3-0. I go into a cricket match expecting to win every game I play, and I never expect to lose."

England's Matthew Hoggard (sledging name: Shrek / Worzel Gummidge) didn't usually air his views in public but he reacted to McGrath's comments with:

"They are always trying to put us down, but the last Test match we played against them we beat them. They like putting themselves in the spotlight and bigging themselves up, but we're second in the world now and very capable of beating them."

As the media and players hyped the coming occasion, the public was catapulted into, according to Harry Pearson of the *Guardian*:

"A contest that has featured some of the loudest rows, fiercest finger-pointing and most unpleasant facial hair in the history of sport."

The latter point was seized upon by Eric Morecombe when he and Ernie Wise entertained Dennis Lillee on a show in the 1970s:

"Are you aware, sir, that the last time I saw anything like that on a top lip, the whole herd had to be destroyed?"

On the first morning of the Lord's Test, Steve Harmison served up some extremely hostile bowling. By the time he'd hit Australian captain Ricky Ponting on the helmet grille (which drew blood and required Ponting to have treatment), he'd already battered Langer's body and hit Hayden on the head. Ponting criticised England's lack of courtesy as no one had stopped to ask if he was alright. Bowler Simon Jones recalls the incident:

"No one wants to see a player hurt but they weren't going to get any sympathy from us. It was about controlled aggression, not going over the top."

Langer approached club-mate and good friend Andrew Strauss to see what he thought of the incident:

"This really is war out here, isn't it? You're not even going to see if he's alright."

Strauss recalls:

"No one said a word."

In England's first innings, Ricky Ponting welcomed opposite number Michael Vaughan to the crease with a number of subtle sledges. Vaughan decided to fight fire with fire:

"Who do you think you are? Steve Waugh? Why don't you get back to the slips?"

Old rivalries were resumed in the 2010-11 Ashes series in Australia. James Anderson and Mitchell Johnson were at each other's throats for most of the first Test but England had the last laugh and Johnson was dropped before the Adelaide Test. Looking for someone else to pick on, the usually reserved Anderson subjected Mike Hussey to a series of tasteless sledges but Mr Cricket was not fazed and went on to average well over 50 in the series.

Johnson was back on the offensive in the third Test in Perth when he was also back to his best with the ball in hand. He demolished the England line-up with nine wickets in the match and then proceeded to hound Andrew Strauss from the pitch with a volley of abuse ringing in his ears. In a rare moment of levity, The Australian media suggested that he might have gone over the top. Kevin Pietersen stepped in to restore order by repeatedly asking for Johnson's phone number. Johnson is said to have replied:

"Stop being such a smart arse."

Pietersen reportedly countered with:

"I don't mean it like that. I don't want a relationship. I play cricket to make friends and I was hoping we could become friends."

Pietersen spoke to the press afterwards, claiming:

"What was said out there will stay out there. I'd just like to add that this lot can't sledge anywhere near as well as Warne and McGrath."

Indeed, Johnson's best effort at sledging Anderson consisted of:

"Why are you chirping at us now, mate? You're not getting any wickets."

Anderson, of course, replied the next ball by clean bowling the Australian and sending him back to the pavilion with a finger to his lips.

THE ENGLISH VIEW

Traditionally, sledging has not played a great part in the development of the English game. We've discussed the impact of the Champion, W.G. Grace, on the sport as it was in its professional and amateur infancy, but his rule-bending was the exception rather than the norm. Indeed it was considered extremely bad form to comment on the skill of an opponent during the course of play. It was just 'not cricket'. As the Ashes battles between England and Australia heated up after the Second World War, and almost mythical status was conferred upon the contest, English players were subjected to the mild sledging that had appeared in the antipodean game. In order to compete, they had to toughen up, both mentally and physically, and sledging became an integral part of the sport at home. Personal abuse is still frowned upon, however, although it is perfectly acceptable to pass judgement on an opposing player's ability, whether that be with the bat or in the field. Former captain Nasser Hussain believes the practice is here to stay, providing it remains within acceptable limits:

"I wouldn't want to see players walking around and not saying anything. Gone are the days when you clapped the next batsman in. Part of the enjoyment of sport is

seeing someone succumb to pressure. I consider sledging as something you say to try to put someone off their game by picking on their weakness, even if it's only by one percent, but I don't believe there should be anything said regarding race or family. Modern test cricket is tough. It's a man's game. If you don't like it, go and do something else."

Andrew Flintoff agrees:

"There's an unwritten rule that you don't go in for personal attacks or random abuse, and if you don't think it's going to have any bearing on how the player will bat or bowl it's not worth it. I only sledge the people I think I can get the edge over and then I'll carry on the banter a little bit."

Ian Botham had a similar opinion:

"I loved sledging, thrived on it, but I'd only sledge someone I thought it would affect. I'd never sledge Border, Waugh or Richards because I didn't want to wake them up. The soft guys are fair game; it's that predator instinct."

THE WEST INDIAN VIEW

The islanders were not interested in jumping on the sledging bandwagon until the 1970s and '80s. They found, in this their period of utter dominance, that opposing players were resorting to the tactic in order to unsettle them. Other teams feared their lethal fast bowlers, particularly Holding, Roberts, Croft, Garner and Marshall, who terrorised batsmen for a generation with their devastating pace. It was a brave man who sledged the West Indians when they knew they would have to face these men without the helmets and body armour that exist today. But there came a point when getting the likes of Viv 'the master blaster' Richards out outweighed the consequences, and the sledging began. They are now well known for holding their own in the battles of wits, although any racial or cultural slurs are viewed as quite unacceptable. Michael Holding recalls that:

"We didn't hear too much being said in my day. Neither the West Indies team I played for, nor the teams that played against us had a lot to chat about. If anything was said, it was never derogatory. You'd hear the odd sarcastic remark but I didn't have a problem with that. If someone gets personal and wants to talk about your family or your race or religion, now that's overstepping the mark."

2
THE WELCOME

If you're an opening batsman there are bound to be a few nerves as you walk to the crease to begin your country's innings in a Test match at Lord's. For those less experienced, you might still feel a flutter in the stomach as you take guard in the annual school house match. But no matter what the occasion, you are likely to receive a welcome to the wicket from opposing players. These might vary from the casual 'oh, he looks a bit nervous' comments found on the school playground to the slightly more sinister welcomes discussed below. Make no mistake however, the intention remains the same: the fielding side is trying to put the batsman off and make sure he gets out cheaply, preferably without troubling the scorers.

Some players will volunteer a reply, others deem this unwise until they have batted long enough to force the fielding side to up the abuse. Here are a few of the classic welcomes issued in the cauldron of the Test and county arena:

England's David Steele was an unlikely hero in the 1975 Ashes series, although he didn't really look the part with his silver hair and spectacles. Aussie fast bowler Jeff Thomson was so surprised by his appearance when he got to the crease that he was heard to remark:

"Who's this then? Father fucking Christmas?"

And he can't have had a very long memory, for when Steele – recalling the incident during the Ashes build-up in 2005 – came back to take guard in the second Test at Lord's, Thommo was heard to shout:

"Who the fuck is this? Groucho Marx?"

Fast bowling partner Dennis Lillee was more direct:

"Steeley, you little shit."

Steele saved his reply for wicketkeeper Rod Marsh as he took guard:

"Take a good look at this arse of mine. You'll be seeing plenty of it this summer."

*

Lancashire batsman Chris Schofield arrived at the wicket to face Yorkshire pace-man Steve Kirby. Kirby noticed that the Lancastrian looked a little nervous and tried to settle his butterflies with:

"Around the wicket, umpire, and call an ambulance."

The key to annoying the bowler here is to avoid being

hit. However, if taking evasive action to the early short-pitched deliveries means you are left scuttling around the crease looking for cover, there are likely to be further tirades of abuse about your technique hurled in your direction. If you can survive the opening hostility and go on to score a few runs, the banter is likely to die down. Kirby was on the offensive again in a match against the touring Australians. As Steve Waugh came to the crease, he welcomed him with:

"We don't want you here. Why don't you just get out and leave the ground?"

Waugh replied:

"Sorry, but this is my favourite pitch. And who are you, the fucking mayor?"

Every time the Australian played and missed, Kirby would steam up and say:

"You're not good enough to be the Australian captain."

To which Waugh would reply:

"Do you bowl the same sort of shit from around the wicket?"

The youngest Waugh brother, Dean, had to be content playing Grade cricket in Australia. He was struggling at the crease against New South Wales bowler Richard

Stobo, prompting the latter to quip:

"You must be adopted."

*

'Fiery' Fred Trueman was another who favoured the early unsettling remark. As any Australian took the field at Lord's, or anywhere with the required gate for that matter, he'd welcome them with:

"Don't bother to shut it, son, you won't be out here long enough."

It is advisable after this introduction not to get out first ball, although against Fred at his best that wasn't always possible. Team-mates recall trying to calm the big Yorkshireman down if he was playing at anything less than Test level. In a friendly he was once asked by his captain, well within earshot of a confident batsman, to:

"Slip him a nice half-volley to get him on his way."

Trueman replied:

"Aye, and with the next ball I'll pin him to the flippin' sight screen."

There are so many stories involving Trueman that it's hard to pick out the best, but this next one makes it in as it gives us an insight into his sarcastic streak. He'd pinned the batsman back against his stumps and a huge LBW appeal had gone up. The umpire was having none of it, even though the batsman looked plumb in front. Fred merely grunted and got on with the job. A few balls later the batsman got a thick edge which the 'keeper took comfortably. To everyone's disbelief the umpire again returned the verdict of 'not out'. Fred grunted and headed back to his mark. The next ball scattered the batsman's stumps to all corners. Cool as you like, Trueman turned to the umpire and said:

"That's got to be bloody close, hasn't it?"

Trueman's views outside the game were almost always controversial, this about women from *A Century of Great Cricket Quotes*:

"You should treat them the same way a Yorkshire batsman used to treat a cricket ball. Don't stroke 'em, don't tickle 'em, just give 'em a ruddy good belt."

*

As Ian Botham took guard in an Ashes Test in 1981 to try and steady the England ship, Australian wicketkeeper Rod Marsh decided to help him settle with the words:

"So, how's your wife and my kids?"

This is an old favourite and has been used many times throughout cricket's rich history, but this occasion was arguably the most famous. Botham, of course, replied with both bat and ball during the series, scoring match-changing runs at Headingley and Old Trafford and demolishing the Aussies with a bowling spell of five wickets for one run in 28 deliveries at Edgbaston in the fourth Test. Of course the verbal reply can be equally as effective:

"The wife's fine but the kids are retarded."

Most commentators when asked now if it is acceptable to involve a player's children in the banter agree that it is not, although one said dryly that:

"It doesn't matter because most Australian players aren't related to their kids."

Another favourite Botham line when he was on the receiving end of an attempted sledge was:

"You Aussies are just like your country: big and empty. You're a bunch of hicks who don't know the first thing about cricket."

Marsh, incidentally, proved he was not just a sledger but a true sportsman when, in the Centenary Test in Melbourne in 1977, he asked the umpire to give England's Derek Randall not out despite him appearing to take a catch behind the stumps. Randall was on 161 at the time and pushing hard for a world record 463 fourth innings total to win the match. Sadly he fell on 174 with England needing just 46 for victory. Early in his innings he'd played and missed at a couple of Lillee out-swingers, prompting the bowler to chirp:

"Just hold the bat still and I'll try and hit it."

Here's another classic sledge (and reply) from that Centenary Test. Inexperienced Australian batsman David Hookes was welcomed to the crease by South African-born Tony Greig with:

"When are your balls going to drop, son?"

"I don't know, but at least I'm playing for my own country.

CROWD TROUBLE

It's not just the players and umpires who end up in the wars of words, the crowds, too, can play a big role in upsetting batsmen and fielders. Here are some of the not so nice chants and barracks.

Somerset supporters taunted portly Kent and England star Colin Cowdrey during a one-day game in the 1970s with this ditty, sung to the tune of 'Deck the Hall with Boughs of Holly':

"Cowdrey is a big fat fairy, fa-la-la-la-la, la-la-la-la."

*

During the 1950-51 tour of Australia, MCC's Warwickshire leg-spinner Eric Hollies was being barracked by the crowd on Sydney Cricket Ground's notorious hill. In answer to their question:

"Don't they bury their dead in Birmingham?"

He replied:

"No, they stuff them and send them out to Australia."

*

During a match in Canada, Pakistan captain Inzamam-ul-Haq confronted a spectator having been called a:

"Fat potato."

Mind you, he was no stranger to confrontation. He once marched up to Aussie pace-man Brett Lee and asked him to:

"Stop bowling off-breaks."

Victorian fast bowler Brad Williams was another who realised it was a bad idea to wake up the bear. He repeatedly sledged Inzamam so the Pakistani captain smashed him for 23 runs the next over and told him he'd need to up his pace considerably (from 95mph!) if he wanted to get him out.

*

And Kent's big-boned batsman Robert Key was often called:

"Bob the Builder."

He was even sledged by a South African opponent about his weight during the Under-19 World Cup in 1998:

"Come on, lads, he's sweating Big Macs out here."

Of course there were plenty more lines fired in his direction:

"You must be the widest English cricketer since Mike Gatting."

"Who ate all the pies?"

*

Sri Lankan off-spinner Muttiah Muralitharan has endured years of speculation over the validity of his bowling action. The English Barmy Army had clearly made up their minds when they penned the words to this song, sung to the tune of 'Row, row, row the boat':

"Throw, throw, throw the ball gently down the seam,
Murali, Murali, Murali, Murali, chucks it like a dream.
Bowl, bowl, bowl the ball gently through the air,

Murali, Murali, Murali, Murali, here comes Darrell Hair.... No ball!"

The Barmy Army like to make as much noise as possible at Test matches, particularly when competing with the notorious Bay 13 crowd at the MCG during the Ashes. When England are in the ascendant, these chants can often be heard:

"Get your shit stars off our flag."

"He's fat, he's round, he bounces off the ground – Shane Warne, Shane Warne."

"Are you Bangladesh in disguise?"

*

During the infamous 'Bodyline' series of 1932-33, England captain Douglas Jardine was given special attention by the crowd with taunts like:

"Don't give the bastard a drink – let him die of thirst."

"Leave our flies alone, Jardine, they're the only friends you've got in Australia."

*

The Australian fans have always been well-known for their Pom-bashing antics. This was directed at Trevor

Bailey in Sydney in the '50s:

"I wish you were a statue and I was a pigeon."

And this was reserved for Bob Willis in 1970, referring to the bowler's tall, lanky frame:

"I didn't know they stacked crap that high."

Phil Tufnell was never going to get away without a mention in this section. Here he comes under fire from a barracker in 1994:

"Can I borrow your brain? I'm building an idiot."

And here he takes one from umpire Peter McConnell after politely inquiring how many balls were left in the over during the second Test in 1990:

"Count them yourself, you Pommie cunt."

Tufnell was flabbergasted, although he was soon celebrating is first Test wicket when David Boon edged the ball to 'keeper Jack Russell. McConnell shook his head at the appeal, so Tufnell berated him with:

"You're a fucking bastard."

In the next Test, Greg Matthews holed out to Eddie Hemmings and Tufnell finally had his wicket. As he celebrated, he ran past McConnell and screamed:

"I suppose that's not out either!"

∗

Dickie Bird managed to stump Dennis Lillee after the bowler had repeatedly appealed for an LBW decision:

"I think your eyesight must be going, Dickie."

"It's your eyesight that's going, Dennis. I'm the ice cream man."

The legendary umpire threatened to 'no ball' Merv Hughes after the bowler had asked him:

"Have I bowled three this over, or are there three to come?"

The players occasionally managed to get one over the umpires, however. In 1948 a stray dog ran onto the pitch. Australian batsman Sidney Barnes managed to catch it and give it to umpire Alex Skelding. The umpire had given Barnes out LBW twice on the tour so he decided to let Skelding know what he thought of his eyesight:

"Now all you need is a white stick."

∗

Former fast bowler Angus Fraser remembers England's James Anderson walking onto the pitch in Melbourne in

2002 wearing a shirt that had no name on it – which was unusual for a one-day game – prompting a fan to shout:

"Hey, Pom, are you too fucking embarrassed to have your name on your shirt?"

Or there's always this reminder about how difficult he found it to force himself into the Test side:

"Shouldn't you be bowling at one stump during the tea break?"

*

Surrey and England's Mark Butcher fielded this one from a Brixton resident in 2005:

"Hey, man, Graham Thorpe, right?"

*

The England fans do manage to get in on the act occasionally. When Australia toured in 1997, they aimed a fair amount of abuse at bowler Jason 'Dizzie' Gillespie over his dishevelled, gypsy-like appearance with:

"Where's your caravan?"

"Glastonbury finished last week."

Aussie team mate Matthew Hayden found himself on the

receiving end from one fan at the SCG in 2005 after the batsman had released his cookbook:

"Hayden, your casserole tastes like shit."

*

During the morning session of a county match in the 1960s (according to the *Telegraph*'s Martin Johnson), an Old Trafford member was heard to shout at Lancashire batsman Harry Pilling, because of his extremely slow play:

"Bloody hell, Pilling, you're still eight not out in the Manchester Evening News."

*

In the deciding Ashes Test at the Oval in 2005, Shane Warne was barracked by the Aussies in the crowd who held up banners saying:

"It ain't over until the fat man spins."

"Fat boy spin."

The Barmy Army tend to take things a step further. This ditty is sung to the tune of the Beatles' Yellow Submarine:

"You all live in a convict colony...."

In another epic home contest against the Australians in 2009, the Barmy Army were once again in full voice. England were leading the series going into the Edgbaston Test so the crowd were chanting:

"Stand up if you're 1-0 up."

"Can we play you every week?"

"It's just like playing Scotland."

Stuart Broad and Mitchell Johnson provided a good deal of on-field banter during the Edgbaston Test. Johnson was getting stuck into Graeme Swann so Broad, who had claimed earlier that he loved the sledging side of cricket because it got him pumped up, marched over and told the fast bowler to:

"Fuck off back to your mark."

Johnson couldn't resist having a final dig at Swann:

"I'll pay you to hit me to the boundary."

Swann duly obliged the next ball and replied with:

"How much change have you got?"

The crowd delighted in the exchange, taunting the Australian bowler with:

"Super, super Mitch, super, super Mitch, super, super Mitch, super Mitchell Johnson!"

And they were quick to leap on young spinner Nathan Hauritz after a miss-field:

"No wonder you couldn't get there in time. Your legs are still chained together."

*

During the West Indies' tour match in Perth in 1997 one of the home supporters held up a banner saying:

"West Indies – Ambrose = Poms."

Ambrose took exception to the sledge and bowled the West Indies to victory.

*

In the final Test match of Pakistan's tour to Australia in 1995, a man in the SCG crowd waited for Salim Malik, a batsman tainted by allegations of match-fixing, to be dismissed before shouting:

"The cheque is in the post."

One sledger who tended to end up on the winning side in the verbal exchanges was Steve Waugh. (His brother,

Mark, incidentally, was known to sledgers and team-mates alike as Afghanistan: the forgotten war.) Every time Nasser Hussain came to the wicket the Aussie would chirp one of two standard lines:

"Enjoy it, Nasser, this is your last Test match. We will never see you again."

"When you're gone, who's going to shore up the middle order with a stodgy 29 off 117 balls?"

During the 1997 Ashes, England realised that sledging the Australian only seemed to make him more determined to succeed with the bat. The hostile atmosphere and snide remarks had little effect. So they decided to ignore him completely in the hope that he would initiate the 'action'. Waugh arrived at the crease to total silence and quipped:

"Oh, so you're not talking to me, are you? Well I'll talk to myself then."

To England's dismay he went on to talk to himself for six hours in the first innings and ten hours in the second!

In the first Test of that series at Edgbaston, Nasser Hussain had come on as a substitute fielder to a tirade of abuse from Aussie batsman Justin Langer, and the Englishman took offence, replying with:

"I don't mind this lot chirping at me but you're just

the fucking bus driver of this team. So you get back on the bus and get ready to drive it back to the hotel this evening."

Justin Langer clearly viewed sledging as an important facet of the game, so much so that he produced a dossier on the English players (and crowds) before the 2009 series:

"English cricketers are great front runners. They will be up when things are going well but they will taper off quickly if you wear them down in all departments. As soon as it gets a bit hard, you'll see how flat and lazy they get. Take them out of their comfort zone and they don't like it. This can be done by aggressive bowling, confident body language and not being too friendly. Ravi Bopara is sure to wind the boys up with his strutting and he thrives on the chat. Anderson can be a bit of a pussy if he is worn down. Swann is also sure to wind us up with his body language and ego. I would chip away at Matt Prior about his wicket-keeping and why his massive ego might see him dropped from the team. The crowd in Cardiff will be feral, brutal and very aggressive, which is something the boys should be aware of."

Shane Warne managed to say the same thing in one line:

"When the pressure point comes, England crumble."

South African Daryll Cullinan was famously inept at

playing Warne and had got out to the master leg-spinner on numerous occasions. He'd even resorted to sessions with a psychologist in an effort to overcome Warne's stranglehold, prompting the Australian to chirp:

"I'm going to send you straight back to the leather couch."

He was out next ball. The two didn't meet again at international level for a couple of seasons. But when they did Warne, never one to shy away from having a word or two with the batsman, welcomed his so-called 'rabbit' back to the crease with:

"I've waited two years for another chance to humiliate you."

Quick as a flashing cover drive, Cullinan replied:

"Looks like you spent it eating."

He'd also previously taunted the Aussie with:

"Leave us some lunch, fat boy."

To which Warne replied:

"What colour was that couch?"

Cullinan, of course, knew that Warne was partial to a pie or two and carried a little extra weight, but he must have known it was a dangerous game to play with the record-breaking spinner and he was dismissed shortly afterwards by a beautiful flipper. In fact Warne didn't even need to be bowling at him for the Aussie to rear his right arm and drop one into the rough. Cullinan was facing New Zealand's Chris Harris in a Test match when he played the spinner's first ball carefully back down the track. Kiwi 'keeper Adam Parore quipped:

"Well bowled, Warnie!"

The man himself was back in action in 2005 against South Africa. Justin Kemp was facing and was struggling to pick Warne's flippers, sliders and googlies, so much so that the spinner started saying, every time Kemp missed:

"Well batted, Daryll."

And if you thought Warne wasn't involved in enough controversy, try these on for size: In 2004 he was alleged to have called England's Ronnie Irani's mother a:

"Whore."

He'd been standing in the slips when Irani marched up to him and the pair began going at it. Supporters heard Irani swearing at the Australian but he replied to this allegation with:

"What would you say to someone if they were standing

behind you calling your mother a whore?"

Warne could have used a slightly more subtle but equally effective line:

"You should be a professional, just like your mother."

When asked about the matter later, the Australian replied diplomatically:

"What was said on the field stays on the field."

Indeed this is one of Warne's fundamental beliefs. He was widely criticised for sledging Matt Prior over the Sussex man's well-developed chest during a county match in 2005 with the comment:

"Watermelons."

Sussex captain Chris Adams was unhappy about the incident but Warne was unrepentant, claiming that he was responding to the pushing of international team mate Simon Katich by Prior. Katich found it so funny that he was unable to bowl the next over. Warne issued this statement afterwards:

"My conscience is clear and I will not apologise for my actions. The only reason you hear about Australians sledging is because we don't say what has happened out on the field. We just have a beer afterwards. If people want to talk about what happens in the middle and they

don't like it, I can't control that, but I'm not going to apologise for it either. Anyone who comes up against me is going to be tested, mentally, physically and technically. If they don't like it, we'll win easily. If I get sledged out in the middle you won't hear me saying what anyone said to me."

The Australian's language hadn't always been that articulate. In 2001 Grant Flower, the Zimbabwean batsman, played Warne away for a couple of runs, to which Warne, standing well within earshot of the stump microphones, shouted:

"You fucking arsey cunt!"

He was also well-known for sledging opposing batsmen with the words:

"You're a fucking dill, softcock."

Warne apparently welcomed New Zealand's Matthew Sinclair to the crease with:

"Fuck off, you buck-toothed cunt."

Sinclair was a little surprised by the outburst, saying in the bar afterwards:

"My teeth may stick out a bit but I hardly know the guy."

And Warne gave South African Gary Kirsten the nickname Tom Cruise after the opener had tried to chat up the wives and girlfriends of the Australian team on their 1993 tour. Kirsten realised his mistake too late and couldn't sleep that night:

"The abuse I was going to get on the field the following day chilled me to the bone."

It was while Warne was batting that he offered one of his best lines. Paul Collingwood had chipped in with a couple of runs at The Oval during the final Ashes Test of 2005 and had been awarded an MBE as part of the victorious team. He was standing at point in the 2006-07 series when he fired a quick line at the batsman. Warne chuckled and looked him squarely in the eye:

"You must have been embarrassed to get an MBE for scoring seven runs."

It's worth noting that Warne can be countered with the odd line:

"You've got another bald spot coming on, Shane."

"You're one of the world's greatest text cricketers."

"Every time I hit you for four you squeal like Maria Sharapova."

"Well bald, Warnie!"

But we'll leave the last word for now about Warne to arch-enemy Daryll Cullinan:

"Why don't you go and deflate yourself, you balloon."

*

A young, bespectacled and inexperienced Geoffrey Boycott was singled out by Australian captain Bobby Simpson as he took guard in the Trent Bridge Test in 1964. The captain pulled bowler Garth MacKenzie to one side and loudly chirped:

"Hey, Garth, look at this four-eyed fucker. He can't fucking bat. Knock those fucking glasses off him straight away!"

And after the first ball:

"Better ease off a bit. This one's still on the tit."

Boycott was England's master accumulator of runs, scoring over 8,000 in Tests by the end of his career, but he was also a master at running out team-mates, and was even heard shouting "sacrifice" to one stranded individual. He famously ran out Nottinghamshire's Derek Randall on his home ground in 1977, which provoked this reaction from Martin Kelner in the *Guardian*:

"Myra Hindley only participated in some of the grisliest murders of the 20th century but Geoffrey ran out Derek

Randall at Trent Bridge."

The following year Boycott was batting so poorly against New Zealand that Botham was given instructions to run him out. He duly did, prompting Boycott to wail:

"What have you done? What have you done?"

Botham is said to have quoted Nelson in reply:

"Thank God I have done my duty."

Randall had his own problems running between the wickets. He'd run three county team-mates out by tea when he was heard to say:

"Sorry, lads, I'm batting like Wally Hammond but running like Charlie Chaplin."

Another controversial run out involving Randall led to one of the game's finest sledges. New Zealander Ewen Chatfield had just run the Nottinghamshire man out while he was backing up at the bowler's end at Christchurch in 1978. It was considered gamesmanship and the usual course of action would have been to warn the batsman that you know he's encroaching down the wicket before taking the bails off if he was out of his ground later on. But Randall walked and Botham reprimanded the Kiwi with:

"Just remember one thing: you've already been killed

once on a cricket field."

This was a gentle reminder to Chatfield that a Peter Lever bouncer had struck him on the head a couple of years earlier and his heart had momentarily stopped. Advantage Botham, you might say. However, this was not the first time a serious injury had occurred on the pitch. Roger Davis was almost killed by a hit on the head in 1971 in an incident that gave rise to the use of protective gear for the close-in fielders and helmets for the batsmen. John Emburey had to clear Warwick Darling's throat after the latter had swallowed his gum after a blow on the chest from Bob Willis, and Frederik, Prince of Wales, is reported to have died of complications from a cricket ball strike in 1751, although how accurate this story is remains open to debate. Raman Lamba was killed by a blow to the head while fielding at forward short leg in Bangladesh in 1998.

But let's get back to Boycott briefly. Having retired from the game the Yorkshireman's strong views would get an airing in the commentary box, including this observation on England bowler Graham Dilley:

"He has Dennis Lillee's action and Denis Thatcher's pace."

Boycott would never shy away from saying what he thought, even when it got him into trouble with the authorities. A favourite line, delivered when a bowler had just sent down a juicy half-volley that had been cracked through the covers for four, was:

"That's rubbish, is that."

During England's 2004 series against the West Indies he was less than impressed with the islanders' bowling attack, quipping:

"Corey Collymore and Adam Sanford wouldn't bowl my mum out."

He was also quite prepared to get stuck into the opposition during Ashes clashes; this from 2005:

"The Aussies have been lording it for eighteen years, crowing about how good they are and suggesting that maybe the Ashes were a waste of time. Now they are trying all kinds of psychological clap-trap to hide the fact that they've been outplayed."

Co-commentator Richie Benaud couldn't listen to an outburst from a colleague without having a go back:

"I think the media here, the public and maybe the England dressing room have started to write off Australia. If so, that would be their second mistake. Their first was not taking the last wicket at Old Trafford."

Benaud in serious mode here. The finest commentator of them all does have a humorous side, however. On observing England's field placings in 1995 he remarked:

"Gatting at fine leg – that's a contradiction in terms."

But Benaud was occasionally on the receiving end of a sledge, most memorably when he was prodding the pitch for what seemed like an age when Tony Lock was ready to begin his run up. Benaud continued 'gardening' as some players liked to call it so Lock steamed in and bowled a vicious bouncer, saying afterwards:

"Tap that one down, you little bastard."

*

Dennis Lillee and Fred Trueman, two of the all-time greats, were never shy about airing their views. Here they offer differing opinions on Boycott, Lillee first:

"He's the only fellow I've ever met who fell in love with himself at a young age and has remained faithful ever since."

And Trueman:

"I know why he bought a house by the sea: so he'll be able to go for a walk on the water."

And Boycott's slow batting also attracted its fair share of criticism, this from Jack Binney in 1978:

"You're doing for cricket what the Boston Strangler did for door-to-door salesmen."

*

He may have been a ferocious competitor on the pitch but Lillee was occasionally known for his sense of humour. He once halted his run up as he approached the crease to bowl at a rotund Mike Gatting to quip:

"Move out of the way, Gatt, I can't see the stumps."

He was almost lost for words, however, having hit England's Derek Randall on the head with a vicious bouncer in the Centenary Test in Melbourne in 1977. The batsman silenced him with:

"No good hitting me there, mate, there's nothing to damage."

The two enjoyed a bit of banter during Randall's epic 174. The Englishman was well-known for being a little eccentric, wandering around the crease fidgeting, adjusting his box and constantly talking to himself. As he avoided another Lillee bouncer he doffed his cap to the Aussie:

"That was a good one, Mr Lillee."

Lillee replied:

"I hate bowling at you. It's so much harder to hit a moving target."

Another stock Lillee line could be wheeled out whenever the batsman was playing and missing. Lillee would march down the wicket and chirp:

"You've got some shit on the end of your bat."

When the batsman lifted it up to have a look, Lillee would add:

"Other end, mate."

*

Once the West Indies had embraced the sledging phenomenon it was difficult to keep them quiet. Here's another gem from Viv Richards. Indian legend Sunil Gavaskar usually opened the batting, but for a Test against the 'Windies' in 1983 he'd dropped down the order to number four. Malcolm Marshall dismissed Anshuman Gaekwad and Dilip Vengsarkar for ducks and in trudged Gavaskar. Richards looked up at the scoreboard, then back at the batsman, and said:

"Man, it doesn't matter when you come in to bat, the score is still zero."

Gavaskar had the last laugh on this occasion and went on to score a fabulous hundred. A similar sledge was aimed at Mark Butcher by Ian Healy during the 1998-99 Ashes. Butcher and Atherton had failed to find their form as the opening pair so Butcher dropped down the order to make way for Alec Stewart. A wicket in the first over brought Butcher to the crease so Healy chirped:

"It's no different at three, is it, Butch?"

But back to Gavaskar briefly. During the third Test against Australia at the MCG in 1981 he and Dennis Lillee were having an ongoing duel between bat and ball, as well as in the verbals department. Gavaskar was on 70 when Lillee appealed for an LBW decision. Gavaskar pointed to the bat to indicate he'd hit the ball and expected umpire Rex Whitehead to believe him. But the decision went Lillee's way and angry words were exchanged between the pair. As Gavaskar trudged back to the pavilion, Lillee sledged him and Gavaskar's patience snapped. He led partner Chetan Chauhan from the field, something he immediately regretted:

"Whatever the provocation, whatever the reason, there was no justification for my action and I realise that I did not behave the way a captain and sportsman should."

Thankfully, Chauhan was persuaded to return by team manager SK Durani and India went on to win the match by 59 runs. Gavaskar was no slouch in the sledging stakes, however. Here he replies to a broadside from Australia's Simon O'Donnell:

"There's no need to try and sledge me. I've heard more sledges than you've had pisses."

*

Someone who didn't have the last laugh while sledging Richards was the New South Wales bowler, Dave Colley. He'd hit Richards on the exposed head, appealed for a catch and the umpire had agreed and raised the finger. Richards stood his ground, pointing to his head. Colley reacted with:

"Listen, you cunt, there's nothing in there. Take a look at the scoreboard and fuck off."

At the close of play the NSW team filed into the dressing room for a drink only to be confronted by a snorting, bare-chested Richards standing in the middle of a makeshift boxing ring. Colley realised his mistake and ran!

*

England's Stuart Broad has been singled out for a good helping of abuse over his youthful looks and fiery temper, although he claims not to listen to it because smiling at the opposition as they lose their cool seems to annoy them more. He remembers South African pace-man Dale Steyn christening him 'Baywatch', although he said it couldn't have had anything to do with his strapping physique. Instead he fired back:

"Do you play dumb or does it come naturally?"

The code of conduct drawn up in 2003 is designed to

outlaw personal abuse but where is that line drawn? Can you criticise someone's weight, their background, their technique? If not, then does the game lose an integral part of its psychological make-up?

THE AUSTRALASIAN VIEW

Sledging's big boom came in the 1970s, with the Chappell sides in particular employing the tactic. There is no doubt that casual abuse is part of Aussie culture, and this extends across the Tasman to New Zealand. There is great sporting rivalry between the two countries, with each vying to outdo one another on every field, from rugby to cricket, basketball, soccer and beyond. This infighting builds a psychological solidity and the players become hardened to the abuse from an early age. The Australians realised that this mental toughness could be used against the softer English. Richie Benaud's sides in the 1960s started the big celebrations when a wicket fell but the captain was thinking more deeply about the game, probing to find an opposing batsman's weakness and then ruthlessly exploiting it. This led to causal banter with their opponents before the Chappell brothers (the Godfathers of sledging according to Nigel Henderson) took it to a new level. In the '90s it was widely accepted, with even the most vicious verbal assault deemed justifiable if the wicket fell. However, with the introduction of stump microphones, the rise in the number of viewer complaints at the language used prompted the governing bodies to issue a code of conduct (the McGrath-Sarwan incident outlined later provoked the biggest response). In 2003, Cricket Australia CEO James Sutherland issued this statement:

"Criticism of Australian cricket has been justified. Over the past twelve months we've had some incidents that have caused significant harm to the game, and that's not able to be measured. If we're going to be true to the spirit of the game and true to our strategy then we must do something about it."

The resulting code of conduct outlawed sledging that constituted personal abuse – with cultural or racial slurs attracting a possible life ban – with other penalties for excessive appealing, dissent and bad language. The umpires have been given the responsibility of reporting bad behaviour, although cameras or microphones that pick up incidents may be used by the authorities after the match. Most of the time this watered down version of the practice stays where it should – on the pitch – with both sides, since Border's retirement at least, happy to share a beer after the game. There are notable exceptions however, such as the Muralitharan 'chucking' incident and the Simon Jones-Matthew Hayden confrontation during a one-day international in 2005. Jones had appeared to shy at the stumps while collecting a push back from Hayden but he inadvertently struck the batsman, which lead to a heated exchange of un-pleasantries, including this from the Australian:

"Fucking idiot. What the fuck was that for?"

3
SOWING THE SEEDS
OF DOUBT

If you survive the first few balls after the welcome, the fielding side will have to resort to alternative ways of getting you out, although you should expect the 'keeper's chirping to continue all afternoon. They will raise doubts about your technique, your susceptibility to getting out to the in-swinger, or your penchant for hooking the fast men off your eyebrows. And you can guarantee that the bowling will test your powers of self-restraint from the off. Shane Warne is the absolute master of goading a batsman into getting himself out. India's Sourav Ganguly was stumped charging down the wicket to smash Warne out of the ground immediately after being told:

"People don't pay to watch you let balls go."

Chalk up another Test victim to the Australian. In the 2005 Ashes contest at Lord's he patted England's Kevin Pietersen on the bum having watched a delivery get smashed into the stands. It was Pietersen's debut and he'd just made a timely fifty at cricket's headquarters to steady the England ship. He even allowed himself a wink at the spin king. Warne, who'd christened Pietersen '600' as he anticipated the Englishman becoming his six hundredth Test victim, simply nodded his approval at his new club mate and said:

"Well batted."

Crafty as ever, Warne gave him the same delivery next ball and Pietersen couldn't resist. Damien Martyn took a brilliant diving catch on the boundary. Warne simply winked back: job done. Later in the series he was batting at number eight and his team were in trouble. Andrew Strauss sensed England were closing in on victory and said:

"Let's wrap this up, fellas. We're into the tail now."

Warne waltzed down the wicket and smashed the next ball for six, then turned to Strauss:

"I don't know what you're talking about."

But if you thought the spinner had it all his own way, think again. South Africa were touring Australia in the mid-'90s and bulky Proteas batsman Brian McMillan was at the crease. The Aussies had decided not to give him too much abuse as he was such a big chap, but he was playing and missing so often that the maestro couldn't resist a quick chirp:

"Hey, Big Mac, I'll call them out to you. Maybe that'll help."

And he proceeded to call out every delivery, whether it was the conventional leg-spinner, the wrong 'un, flipper or slider. As it happened McMillan still couldn't find the middle of the bat and he became increasingly irate. After being tormented for about four overs, he marched down the wicket to Warne and said:

"Hey, Shane, you know you're coming to South Africa next month. Well, hundreds of people go missing in our country every day. Perhaps I'll take you shark fishing and use you as bait."

For once Warne seemed genuinely shocked and his bowling fell to pieces. At the end of the next over he shuffled off to the slips saying:

"Do you think he meant it?"

More often than not, however, Warne was head and shoulders above the other players in the abuse stakes. England's Andrew Strauss was another who was on the receiving end of some psychological sledging. The Aussie had told the opener in a Middlesex-Hampshire match early in the 2005 season:

"You will be my next 'rabbit', my new Daryll."

And he was also targeted with lines like:

"Are you going to take guard, Lord Brocket, or does your butler do it for you?"

Strauss recalls that:

"We knew the Australians would try and get under our skins but we decided not to get lured into a slanging match."

Strauss survived that innings but Ian Bell was not so lucky in the first Test. He'd had a superb series against Bangladesh and his batting average was 297, but he'd yet to face the likes of McGrath and Warne. He recalls one of the comments, this from noted bully Matthew Hayden:

"Oh dear, is that how you're going to play Shane Warne?"

The Australians deliberately targeted Bell, nicknaming him 'The Sherminator' after the geek in the *American Pie* films, and Bell was forced to admit that the tourists had got to him. He was apparently called 'The Bisto Kid with the face of a ferret', too. Bell noted that Warne's tactics didn't always revolve around sledging, however. The Australian was a master of the mind games too:

"He plays a mental game with you, slowing things down, waiting at his mark and then rushing you. It was an education."

He eventually padded up to a ball that went straight on and was given out LBW. Glenn McGrath was quick to seize on another opportunity to punish the Englishman:

"Shane set him up perfectly with a couple that really turned and then he slipped in the slider. The same thing had happened when he bowled at Bell in a county match, except then it only took two balls."

Even when McGrath couldn't make the side due to injury, he made sure his deputy was fully prepared for the war of words. In the 2005 Ashes series the Aussie pace-man suffered an elbow injury before the fourth Test at Trent Bridge and Shaun Tait, a young, tearaway fast bowler, was called in as cover. Tait had clearly been taking lessons from his mentor in the verbal department:

"I don't set out to kill anyone, but I do need to hit a few... if there's blood, that should frighten off the others."

England, of course, went on to win that Test by three wickets and the series had come along way from where Australian captain Ricky Ponting had seen it after the opening Test at Lord's. He'd been delighted after his team's initial triumph, saying:

"I wouldn't say we've destroyed their confidence, but we've gone some way towards doing that."

Former Test umpire Lou Rowan was less than impressed with the Australian captain's behaviour – particularly the sledging – and loosed this outburst via Fox Sports:

"Ponting is a smart-arse and a disaster as leader. The conduct of him and his players is absolutely disgraceful.

It is an insult to former players and people associated with the game."

Rowan made his comments after hearing that the Australians had apparently been targeting Harmison about his homesickness on the previous tour:

"You must be allergic to your passport."

"You travel about as well as an unstable real ale."

"QUANTAS are having a summer sale."

"You've got as much never-say-die as a kamikaze pilot."

But it's relatively easy to fire one back at Ponting:

"You're the most disastrous leader since George W Bush."

"Are you the only man to have captained three Ashes-losing sides?"

*

Tall Middlesex spinner John Emburey had dismissed Glamorgan's Hugh Morris, Tony Cottey and Alistair Dalton, all of whom were around 5'6", when in walked strapping six-footer Steve Barwick. Emburey looked over to captain Mike Gatting and chirped:

"Fuck me, this must be Snow White."

From then on, whenever the shorter Glamorgan players were fielding on the boundary, the crowds would taunt them with:

"Hi ho, hi ho, it's off to work we go."

*

England were cruising to victory in a one-day international in Sydney in 1999, with captain Nasser Hussain guiding them home. Shane Warne waited for him to hit a big six before chirping:

"That's the way to do it, Nass, but it's crucial not to get out now and let your team-mates down."

A couple of balls later, Hussain tried the same shot and was stumped by Gilchrist. England immediately collapsed and Australia won by ten runs.

*

It doesn't happen as often but occasionally the batsman gets the first word in. This is not always sensible because the player then opens himself up to a torrent of abuse from the fielders while he should be concentrating on accumulating the runs. Javed Miandad found this out to his cost when, during the 1991 Test between Pakistan and Australia at Adelaide, he squared up to the Victorian pace-man, big Merv Hughes, calling him a:

"Fat bus conductor."

Hughes had his revenge a few balls later and, while passing the departing batsman, shouted:

"Tickets please!"

Miandad had another famous run-in, this time with Dennis Lillee in 1981, when he took aim at the Australian with his bat and tried to decapitate him having been kicked up the backside by the bowler. He missed, but the incident did little to ease the tension between the two countries. Barry Norman, incidentally, described Miandad as 'the biggest pain in cricket's arse' in 2003.

*

With Australia closing in on victory in a Test against England in the '50s, their players surrounded the tail-end batsman, one F.S. Trueman, their shadows falling across the pitch. Trueman objected of course:

"If you buggers don't back off, I'll appeal for bad light."

*

When Neil McKenzie came to the crease for South Africa against Australia, he was careful not to touch any of the white paint or look at his batting partner. Bowler Brett Lee remembered the batsman was extremely superstitious and decided to lay a trap. As McKenzie scrambled for a quick single, he chirped:

"You just touched the line, mate. That's going to bring you bad luck."

McKenzie was clearly unnerved and was later out for 99.

*

In a Sheffield Shield match in the mid-1990s Dean Jones was annoyed that a young upstart bowler was giving him abuse, so he challenged the novice with:

"Do you know who you're talking to?"

The young bowler nodded:

"The biggest cunt in Australian cricket."

*

One man with the ability to back himself against the best bowlers, at least for a time, was Australian opener Matthew Hayden. He walked out to the middle against Pakistan in 2002 and faced a couple of overs from the quickest bowler in the world, Shoaib Akhtar, who was capable of bowling at over a hundred miles an hour.

Once he'd settled in, got off the mark and was flaying Akhtar to all parts of the ground he quipped:

"Is that as fast as you can bowl?"

But Hayden and his colleagues took their verbal assault too far when they came up against South Africa in captain Graeme Smith's first Test series. Hayden waited while the opener made his way to the crease, then asked him:

"How the fuck are you going to handle Shane Warne when he's bowling into the rough? You are no fucking good whatsoever. All Warne does is call you a cunt all day."

Smith revealed what had been said and this precipitated an outburst from the rest of his team, who recounted their own stories of bullying from the middle. The media went into overdrive, with the South African press giving the Australian team a roasting and the Australian camp spinning their lines to minimise the damage. The Aussies were eventually forced to contribute to the 2003 document entitled: The Spirit of Cricket. It's mission statement:

"We do not condone or engage in sledging or any other conduct that constitutes personal abuse. We view positive play, pressure, body language and banter between opponents and ourselves as legitimate tactics and integral parts of the competitive nature of cricket."

*

It's rare that the Australians are on the receiving end of a good riposte but that's what happened to Glenn McGrath when he slipped in one from the 'unexpected questions' file to Zimbabwean number eleven batsman Eddo Brandes. Brandes had played and missed at the pace-man so McGrath politely enquired:

"Oi, Brandes, why are you so fat?"

With lightning mental reactions, Brandes stumped the bowler:

"Because every time I fuck your wife she gives me a biscuit."

The Australian slip cordon reportedly fell about laughing. Chalk one up for Brandes. Ricky Ponting and Damien Martyn managed to see the funny side of another sledge aimed at one of their players in 2005. Shane Watson felt the wrath of the quick reply when he squared up to Kevin Pietersen in an England-Australia one-day international. Watson started giving the Englishman some stick having just watched the ball sail over the boundary rope for six. Pietersen responded to the verbal assault with:

"You're just upset because no one loves you anymore."

This may seem like a fairly innocuous quote, but Watson had just been dumped by his fiancé for, according to one source, someone who was:

"6'6", good-looking and hung like a rogue elephant."

Both Ponting and Martyn acknowledged the quality of the sledge with a quiet chuckle while Watson trudged back to deep fine leg.

*

McGrath, brilliant bowler though he is, and master sledger he can be, often walks into the trap where the intended victim cuts him back down to size, the obvious example having been stated above. But there was another occasion, in 2003, which ended in the most foul-mouthed assault ever heard on the pitch, that aimed at West Indian batsman and vice-captain Ramnaresh Sarwan. (This outburst resulted in the drawing up of a code of conduct for Australian players as it was picked up by cameras and stump microphones. See: The Australian View.) There is an interesting background to the story as the West Indies had been set a world record 418 to win the fourth Test in Antigua. They began poorly and were soon reduced to 50 for two, but Brian Lara and then Shivnarine Chanderpaul and Ramnaresh Sarwan steadied the ship and began to fight back, the latter two going on to make centuries. West Indies lost a few wickets towards the end but held on to win a remarkable match by three wickets. It was during this innings that the spat occurred, so let's take a moment now to enjoy Sarwan's reply to McGrath's question:

"So what does Brian Lara's dick taste like, mate?"

"Why don't you ask your wife?"

Little did Sarwan know that McGrath's wife had been diagnosed with breast cancer and was receiving treatment at the time. The Australian bowler was incensed, yelling:

"If you ever fucking mention my wife again I will fucking rip your fucking throat out!"

He then complained to umpire Shepherd about the West Indian's comment. The words pot, kettle and black spring to mind.

*

And you wouldn't have thought that Shane Warne could also fall into a trap, but he came unstuck when he enquired about long-time adversary Arjuna Ranatunga with:

"He's probably bulked up to around a hundred and fifty kilos at the moment. Swallowed a sheep or something, has he?"

Ranatunga, of course, knew that Warne had tested positive for banned substances so countered:

"It's better to swallow a sheep or a goat than to swallow

what he's been swallowing."

Warne received a one-year ban having tested positive for the diuretic Moduretic, which increases the body's production of urine and aids weight loss. Warne claimed it was given to him by his mother in an effort to improve his appearance (an excuse that was ridiculed by Dick Pound of the doping commission who said it was right up there with "I caught it from the toilet seat"). The drug itself is commonly used by boxers who are struggling to make their weight before a fight, and by jockeys to help their mount last a race. The Australian returned to the Test arena with a point to prove and slipped back into the groove immediately. Come the 2005 Ashes he was back to his bamboozling best. He'd also perfected the backhanded compliment sledge as England pace bowler Simon Jones found out. The tail-ender had joined Andrew Flintoff at the crease in the second Test at Edgbaston and was swinging the bat wholeheartedly at anything the Aussies could serve up. In fact, he was proving a useful foil to the big Lancastrian at the other end. Warne, who had not been able to find the killer ball, quipped to Jones:

"You're playing pretty well, mate. You should bat up the order instead of Strauss."

The two batsmen refused to buckle and let their shots do their talking. Flintoff's fifty came up with a huge six off Michael Kasprowicz, in an over that cost twenty runs, as he and Jones plundered fifty-one runs in just forty minutes. Flintoff's match total of nine sixes easily surpassed Ian Botham's Ashes record of six. Flintoff is no stranger to dishing out the sledging either. While fielding at slip against the West Indies in 2004, he kept giving Tino Best stick for trying to smash Ashley Giles out of the ground. Having watched the batsman have another failed slog, he chirped:

"Mind the pavilion windows, Tino."

Best couldn't resist and danced down the wicket to Giles's next delivery. He swung wildly at it, missed, and was stumped by Geraint Jones. Flintoff reportedly laughed so hard that he gave himself a stitch. He was on the offensive again when Dwayne Bravo was chirping in his ear that Fidel Edwards was going to clean him up during England's innings:

"Let's see where you are in three years, Dwayne, because it certainly won't be out here. This game has got a funny way of biting you up the arse."

Flintoff also engaged in a battle of wits with Kent's Cambridge-educated batsman Ed Smith (a.k.a Hugh Grant to some sledgers) during a county match in 2003:

"Let's get Ed out so he can go beagling on the downs."

"You don't know what beagling is, Fred."

"Then we'll have to get you out so you can go punting

on the Cam."

Of course you can always try and get one up on the all-rounder with a couple of useful lines:

"Freddie, you bat like a barbecue at Wayne Rooney's house: refinement isn't an issue."

"What's the significance of the ear stud, big boy?"

"You're a genuine all-rounder, mate. You're mediocre at more than one discipline."

*

Several Surrey fielders found themselves creasing up as new batsman Ed Giddins was sledged with:

"Can I have a snort leg for this guy please?"

Giddins had tested positive for cocaine and had been given a two-year ban by the ECB, and the Surrey bowler was offering a simple reminder by craftily rearranging the field.

Because of his name, Gloucestershire's Jon Lewis was another player who was easy to sledge:

"I've heard of Jon Lewis: expensive and crap at delivering."

*

South African fast bowler André Nel is well known for his foul-mouthed rants and was described thus by Matthew Norman:

"As a bowler he looks mediocre; as a sledger he stands alone."

Nel was caught smoking marijuana on the 2001 tour of the West Indies and pulled over for drink-driving in Australia in 2003, prompting some opposing players to wait for him to lose his temper before sledging him with:

"Chill out, André. Have a drink and a spliff."

During the first Test against India in 2006 Nel pointed to his heart while bowling at Shanthakumaran Sreesanth (suggesting that the batsman had no courage for ducking a bouncer). Sreesanth replied in the best way possible by charging down the track and smashing his next delivery for six. The Indian batsman then performed a victory dance around the hapless Nel.

WHEN YOUR OWN TEAM-MATES SLEDGE YOU

It doesn't happen very often but sometimes your own team can get frustrated with the way you're playing. If that happens, you'd better be prepared for a large helping of abuse, as this next group discovered.

MCC captain Johnny Douglas chastised all-rounder Percy Fender with this line before the tourists had even landed in Australia for the 1920-21 Ashes series:

"There is no man in England whose bowling I would rather face than yours and no batsman in England I would rather bowl against either."

*

Brian Close was getting fed up with Geoff Boycott's slow play in the 1965 Gillette Cup Final at Lord's, so, according to Martin Kelner in the *Guardian*, he decided to offer the Yorkshireman some advice:

"Next bloody ball, bloody belt it, or I'll wrap your bat round your bloody head."

Fred Trueman had similar views about batting with Boycott:

"At least you'll never die of a stroke, Boycs."

And he couldn't keep his opinion of Ian Botham to himself either:

"He couldn't bowl a hoop down a hill."

*

Dennis Lillee almost came to blows with national team captain Kim Hughes during a net session in the early 1980s. He was angry that the team was performing poorly and blamed a number of blunders on Hughes. As he fired down a fierce bouncer, Hughes was forced to take evasive action, so Lillee asked:

"Did that one hit you?"

"No, I'm okay."

"Watch out for next one then, you bastard."

*

Captain David Gower and bowler Chris Cowdrey were discussing field placements in a Test match against India in Calcutta in 1985. Gower wondered if Mike Gatting should be moved and asked:

"Do you want Gatt a foot wider?"

Cowdrey replied:

"No, he'd burst."

Gatting was on the receiving end again after Shane Warne's 'ball of the century' bamboozled him in the air before clipping the top of off stump at Old Trafford in 1993. Former captain Graham Gooch quipped:

"If it had been a cheese roll, it never would have got past."

And journalist Martin Johnson chipped in with:

"How anyone can spin a ball the width of Gatting boggles the mind."

David Gower was targeted with the occasional one-liner after the disastrous 1989 Ashes tour:

"You should step down in favour of Ken Dodd."

*

Even the world's finest batsman managed to incur the wrath of a team-mate. Warwickshire's Dermot Reeve said to Brain Lara while they were playing against Nottinghamshire in 1995:

"You're turning into a prima donna."

Reeve was sometimes on the receiving end, however. This was said by county rival but England colleague

David Lloyd at Old Trafford in 1995:

"I don't like you, Reeve. I never have. You get right up my nose and if you come anywhere near me, I'll rearrange yours."

Let's give Reeve the last word here though. This was apparently aimed at England team-mate Ian Botham after 'Beefy' had dismissed him in a county game in 1990:

"You're a fat has-been."

*

Now you wouldn't have thought your country's committee chairman would struggle to remember you. Better ask fast bowler Devon Malcolm after Ted Dexter was heard to remark:

"Who could forget Malcolm Devon?"

Dexter had a run in with Sussex and England batsman, the Reverend David Shepherd, after a number of run out decisions went against them in 1963:

"They say the fool of the family always goes into the church."

And Fred Trueman was equally unhappy with Shepherd's catching on the MCC tour of Australia the same year:

"Pretend it's a Sunday, Shep, and put your bloody hands together."

*

Australia's Ian Healy enjoyed getting stuck into the English batsman from his position behind the stumps but occasionally he'd have a go at one of his own. This was aimed at Shane Warne in 1996:

"His idea of a balanced diet is a cheeseburger in each hand."

And the captain of a young Warne's Melbourne club side, Mike Tamblyn, once sledged the novice with:

"You just haven't got it, son."

While playing for their state sides, Warne noticed that compatriot Michael Slater was having a few problems with his bowling so he quietly chirped "tick tock, tick tock" as if suggesting the batsman was about to explode.

*

Former England captain Mike Brearley has been on the receiving end of some abuse too, and not just from the touring Australians. Here Mike Selvey recalls Nancy, the Middlesex tea lady, taking offence to Brearley's request for lighter lunches:

"Tell you what, Michael, I won't tell you how to flippin' bat and you won't tell me how to flippin' cook. All right?"

*

England's Derek Pringle saved a few choice words for Ashley Giles before the 2005 Ashes battle, first on his bowling, then on his batting. The England spinner's action had been likened to the trundling motion of a wheelie-bin, and Australian Terry Alderman was saying how if anyone got out to Giles they should go and hang themselves, so the Englishman hardly needed to hear:

"Only his mother would describe him as an athlete."

"He's part Wally Hammond, part sitting duck."

Giles, now known by sledgers and team-mates alike as Juan Carlos after commemorative mugs for his 2004 benefit season appeared with the misprint 'King of Spain' rather than 'King of Spin', can also be riled by standard lines like:

"Milk turns quicker than your bowling."

"I've got more chance of being hit by space debris than being done in the flight by one of your arm balls."

And Giles's long-time number two, Gareth Batty, simply can't escape:

"You must be the Queen of Spain."

∗

Even football's greats can have momentary slip-ups. Bobby Robson managed to upset a few in the cricket family when he announced this list of sporting legends to appear in 2005:

"We've got a great list of cricketers joining us: Gary Sobers, Ian Botham, Graham Gooch, Alec Stewart, Mike Atherton, Saddam Hussain..."

∗

We've looked at a few of Allan Border's outbursts, both to team-mates and the opposition. Here's a nice line dished out to colleague Craig McDermott after his bowler had asked to change ends at Taunton in 1993:

"Hey, hey, hey! I'm fucking talking to you. Come here, come here, come here. Do that again and you're on the next plane home, son. What was that? You fucking test me and you'll see."

∗

And here's a classic from England captain Mike Atherton; this delivered to Graham Thorpe after the latter had dropped Australian opener Matthew Elliot in the crucial Headingley Test in 1997:

"Congratulations, Thorpey, you've just cost us the Ashes."

Elliot, incidentally, went on to make 199 after England had been dismissed for just 172. Atherton, too, occasionally fielded a sledge from one of his own players, this from Angus Fraser:

"You naturally mistime the ball."

*

This next story has been attributed to both Frank Tyson (the Northamptonshire pace-man who quoted Shakespeare to the opposing batsmen to put them off) and Fred Trueman, but the weight of evidence suggests that the Yorkshireman was responsible. He was bowling to one of Pakistan's batsmen when the ball glanced off the outside edge and flew towards Raman Subba Row standing at first slip. It was a hot day and Row didn't pick the ball up, letting it burst through his hands and then fly between his legs. At the end of the over he sheepishly approached Trueman and said:

"Sorry, Fred, I should have closed my legs."

Trueman, none to happy at the situation, replied:

"No, you bastard, your mother should have."

Australian wicketkeeper Ian Healy had one of the loudest mouths. Just after the introduction of stump microphones, and clearly just before players were warned about using bad language anywhere near them, Healy was heard to have a go at Sri Lankan batsman Arjuna Ranatunga, who had just called for a runner on a particularly warm night in Sydney:

"You don't get a runner for being an overweight, unfit, fat cunt!"

And there's not much you can say to that. Ranatunga had his revenge with the bat so Healy chirped up again in a final effort to get him out. This time the Sri Lankan was waiting:

"You look tired, mate. Why don't you go and lie down."

"I did enough of that last night with your wife."

The hostility between Healy and Ranatunga continued throughout the Sri Lankan's innings because the Aussies still couldn't get him out. Shane Warne was heard to ask the 'keeper for his suggestions on how to remove the portly batsman, particularly how he could draw him out of his crease. Healy replied:

"Put a Mars Bar on a good length. That should do it."

Ranatunga is said to have pointed at David Boon at short leg and replied:

"Don't bother, Boonie will be onto it well before I can move."

Of course there were other ways of sledging the Tasmanian who reportedly drank 52 cans of beer on a Sydney-London flight before the 1989 Ashes:

"That amount of beer would have qualified you as a teetotaller on one of our tours."

"You must be a Merv Hughes Russian babushka doll."

*

Healy was also the master of the quick chirp. Here's his response (quoted in *Spin* magazine) to his captain's suggestion that they place a fielder right under Nasser Hussain's nose:

"That could mean anywhere within three miles."

South African wicketkeeper Mark Boucher had clearly studied the Healy method when he welcomed Zimbabwean batsman Tatenda Taibu to the crease:

"You don't want to get out straight away because your average is only in single figures on this tour, but if you do I'll walk you back to the changing room. What is your tour average anyway? Nine? Nine point five? Okay, we'll round it up and give you ten. Let's see if you can do better than that."

The sledging must have worked because Boucher caught Taibu the next over. Another nice sledge aimed at the Zimbabweans can be asked of any opening batsman:

"Have the rest of the team padded up?"

Australian 'keeper Tim Zoehrer fired a lovely sledge back at Philippe Edmonds during an Ashes match in the 1980s after the England spinner had asked who he was:

"At least I have an identity. You're just Frances Edmonds' husband."

On the subject of wicketkeepers, it was a brave man who sledged Australian Adam Gilchrist, a wrecking ball with the bat who could destroy just about any bowling attack. But a few lines could be wheeled out to unsettle him early on:

"You must be the love-child of Gollum and Martin Clunes."

"Message for Gilchrist: Andy Caddick would like his ears back."

*

The evidence so far suggests that the Australians are the past masters at the art of initiating mental disintegration – indeed it has been said that they have three national team sports: cricket, rugby and Pom bashing – but they have been on the receiving end a few times. West Indian pace bowler Malcolm Marshall, famous for having smashed England's Mike Gatting on the nose with a near-lethal bouncer, was heard to remark to Australian David Boon after the batsman had played and missed a couple of times:

"Now, David, are you going to get out or am I going to have to bowl around the wicket and kill you?"

Marshall was on equally abrasive form when former England captain Ray Illingworth came out of retirement aged fifty to try to help his beloved Yorkshire survive the 1983 season. As he walked out to face Marshall, the fearsome speedster noticed he wasn't wearing a helmet:

Marshall: *"Why aren't you wearing a lid, Illy?"*

Illingworth: *"I've never worn one, mate, and I'm not scared of you."*

Marshall: *"I'll make sure I bowl you out instead of bounce you out then."*

Aussie Mark Waugh was also put in his place having quipped to England's Jimmy Ormond in an Ashes match:

"Mate, what are you doing out here? There's no way you're good enough to represent your country."

Ormond replied:

"Maybe not, but at least I'm the best player in my family."

Waugh, fielding at second slip, had another go at ending an exchange on the winning side when Kiwi Adam Parore came to the crease a few seasons later. The New Zealander played and missed at his first ball prompting Waugh to observe:

"Oh, I remember you from a couple of years ago in Australia. You were shit then and you're fucking useless now."

Parore couldn't resist sending the insult back with interest:

"Yes, that was me, and when I was there you were going out with that ugly old slut, and now I hear you've married her. You dumb cunt."

And one Australian twelfth man also incurred the wrath of the opposition; this time it was India's Ravi Shastri, who famously became only the second man – after Gary Sobers – to hit six sixes in an over in first class cricket. Shastri played a stroke and looked for a quick single, and the substitute fielder, having easily gathered the ball, opened the exchange with:

"If you leave the crease I'll break your fucking head."

Shastri stared at him calmly and replied:

If you could bat as well as you talk you wouldn't be the fucking twelfth man."

＊

England's Peter Richardson was knocked to the ground by a vicious bouncer from South Africa's Peter Heine in 1957. He expected some sympathy from the bowler but was instead helped back to his feet with:

"Get up; I want to hit you again."

＊

This next sledge has passed into myth. The sledger himself denies he said it, but something passed between the two men and it wasn't an exchange of pleasantries. South Africa were cruising to victory over bitter rivals Australia in the latter stages of the 1999 World Cup at Headingley. Australian captain Steve Waugh was trying to steady the ship and was at the crease unbeaten on 56. Then he came unstuck, pushing the ball in the air to Herschelle Gibbs for an easy catch. Gibbs will want to forget what happened next. He started celebrating before he had the ball under control and dropped it. Never one to miss an opportunity to kick someone who is down and out, Waugh is said to have said:

"How does it feel to have dropped the World Cup?"

The Australian captain then went on to make a majestic 120, steering his side to what had seemed an improbable victory. A few days later they beat Pakistan in the final to win the World Cup. Waugh, however, denied the quote, which may have become exaggerated. He claimed he said:

"Looks like you've dropped the match."

A fact that appears to have been borne out. And he was no stranger to the more challenging confrontation when he squared up to West Indian 'quick' Curtly Ambrose in Trinidad in 1995. Ambrose was the most feared bowler in the world at the time and after every ball he would take a couple of paces towards Waugh and stare him down. The Australian grew tired of the game and quipped:

"What the fuck are you looking at?"

Brave words indeed to Ambrose, who replied with:

"Don't you cuss me, man."

According to his autobiography Waugh hadn't the presence of mind to think of saying anything other than:

"Why don't you go and get fucked?"

Ambrose had to be restrained by team-mate Richie Richardson. Waugh continued to court controversy until his last Test, that against India in Sydney in 2004. Here

Parthiv Patel taunted him with:

"So this is your last Test. Let's hear some of that famous sledging of yours."

Waugh replied:

"Show some respect. When I made my Test debut, you were still in nappies."

And here's another classic Waugh sledge. He'd taken a few minutes settling at the crease, checking the field and taking guard in a Sheffield Shield match, when slip fielder Jamie Siddons quipped:

"For Christ's sake it's not a Test match."

To which Waugh replied:

"Of course it isn't; you're playing."

✱

Australian-raised fast bowler Martin McCague must have known he was going to take some stick during England's 1994-95 Ashes tour, but he can't have known he'd be welcomed to the crease with:

"This must be the first case of the rat joining the sinking ship."

*

In a Yorkshire versus Oxford University match, Yorkshire's wicketkeeper Don Brennan was heard to sledge the batsman with this comment to his bowler, Johnny Wardle:

"Don't get him out just yet, Johnny, he smells so bloody lovely."

*

England wicketkeeper Steve Rhodes somehow managed to get a copy of the recording of Australian Michael Bevan's late-night rendezvous with an unnamed woman in a hotel room before an Ashes warm-up match in 1994. As Bevan came to the crease, Rhodes hit the play button on the machine in his pocket. Bevan was so surprised to have the episode replayed to him that he only lasted three balls.

*

India's little maestro Sachin Tendulkar let his bat do the talking on this occasion in 1989. The sixteen-year-old had hit Pakistan's Mustaq Ahmed for two sixes in the previous over when legendary spinner Abdul Qadir challenged him with:

"Why are you hitting the kids? Try and hit me."

Here's how Qadir's over went: 6, 0, 4, 6, 6, 6
Enough said.

＊

Next up is a selection of psychological taunts issued by Sri Lanka's wicketkeeper Kumar Sangakkara, who has quickly become a leading authority on the art of getting people out by any means. In November 2003 England were touring Sri Lanka having selected Gareth Batty as their main spinner. Sangakkara was heard to quip, while Batty was bowling at him:

"Who's your spinner on this tour?"

He saved these outbursts for South Africa's Shaun Pollock:

"We don't complain when we lose away. We don't cry like you did in Morocco, saying 'these are not good conditions'. And then you went to the press conference and said the same thing. Fucking joke. If you win, be gracious. Otherwise it's shit. Graceful, Shaun. Learn it."

"The weight of all the expectation, fellas; weight of the country, chaps; forty-two million supporters right here, Shaun."

Pollock wasn't the only South African to feel the barbs. Ashwell Prince and the other black players reportedly ate at different tables to the white players, prompting Sangakarra to observe:

"Why don't your team mates eat with you, Ash? Don't they think you're good enough for them? Don't they like you? What did you do?"

This was saved for Prince's countryman Andrew Hall:

"Where's the attitude now? Where's the arrogance? Are you guys rattled? Self-doubt, eh?"

Sangakarra was also quick to have a go at India's spinner Harbhajan Singh, otherwise known as The Turbanator, over his bowling action, which had just been reported to the International Cricket Council (ICC):

"Why is it that you bat with a half-sleeve shirt and bowl with a full-sleeve shirt?"

Singh was at the centre of another controversial moment when he and mixed-race Australian Andrew Symonds came to verbal blows during a tour match at the SCG in 2008. He allegedly called Symonds a monkey and was banned by the ICC, although he denied making the comment and the ban was revoked on appeal. To his credit, Symonds said that it was he who had instigated the confrontation, but that didn't stop team-mate Matthew Hayden describing Harbhajan as:

"an obnoxious little weed"

England's Allan Lamb was quick to jump on the Australians for making such a fuss about the incident:
"I simply can't believe the Australians are moaning about Harbhajan's sledge. I mean they are the worst, the absolute worst when it comes to having a sledge."

During that year's Indian Premier League season, Singh once again made the headlines for the wrong reasons. He was angry that Punjab fast bowler Sreesanth was sending his men back to the pavilion in an aggressive manner so when the teams came to shake hands at the end he slapped the bowler in the face, for which he was fined and banned.

*

In England's match against India at Trent Bridge in 2007 the hosts were sliding towards defeat when Zaheer Khan spotted a jelly bean on the ground at short leg as he took guard. He knocked it away with his bat and then edged his first ball to the boundary. This prompted some of England's close fielders to have a quiet word while yet more of the little sweets appeared on the square. Khan lost his temper and began waving his bat the fielding side, who he assumed were having a go at him about his weight.

"I didn't know where they were coming from and maybe I picked on the wrong fielder but this is a serious game and I felt it was insulting."

Paul Collingwood observed afterwards:

"I think he prefers the blue ones to the pink ones."

Of course in the next match in the series, jelly beans were thrown onto the pitch in huge numbers by the Barmy Army.

*

While David Lloyd was playing a club match for Accrington, the Todmorden wicketkeeper was giving him a bit of abuse over his pundit's position with Sky Sports. Lloyd promptly carted the Todmorden off-spinner for successive sixes and turned to the 'keeper:

"Go and ask your bowler what it's like to be smashed out of the ground by a pensioner."

He was on the offensive again during his comeback when another opposition player sledged him with:

"You were no good then and you'll be no good now."

To which Lloyd replied:

"At least you know who I am."

THE SOUTH AFRICAN VIEW

Regardless of the sport, be it rugby, cricket or soccer, all South African sides are mentally tough; it is in their nature. And they have had to rise above the curse of apartheid, for which they still get slated on the pitch, particularly by the Australians. Indeed sledging them over the reported segregation of black and white players while on tour has become a major issue, although some would say that it actually helped the team to bond once the facts were leaked. Captain Graeme Smith's reaction to the Hayden taunts suggests that although the South Africans will take a certain amount, they will not tolerate what they consider to be excessive abuse. During the Hayden tirade, Smith repeatedly looked to Rudi Koertzen for help but the umpire merely shrugged as if he should have been prepared. Smith has become embroiled in a number of high-profile spats with opposition players, most notably with England captain Michael Vaughn and Australians Shane Warne and Ricky Ponting.

For some South Africans, however, the physical confrontation and mental battle were all part of the challenge. When Allan Donald was asked to recount his almighty contest with Mike Atherton he said:

"For me it was the pinnacle of my career to have a real scrap with another scrapper. As long as you don't overstep the mark, I've got no problem with it. You certainly can't take your natural aggression away because that would be stupid."

HAVING A POP IN THE PRESS

If you can't find the time on the field, or your fixture list means you won't meet your nemesis for a while, you can always sledge an opponent through the press. Let's enjoy some of the magic moments culled from the daily papers.

Here Aussie Steve Waugh offers his opinion on Indian captain Sourav Ganguly (Source: *Wisden Cricketers' Almanack* 2004):

"He's a prick, basically, and that's paying him a compliment."

*

Fred Trueman let everyone know how he felt about the appointment of Tony Greig to the England captaincy in the 1970s with:

"There's only one head bigger than Tony Greig's, and that's Birkenhead."

Greig of course was responsible for one of the biggest blunders in sporting history when, before the 1976 Test series against the West Indies, he claimed that:

"If the West Indies are on top they are magnificent. If they are down, they grovel and I intend to make them grovel."

The Windies' fast bowling attack demolished England and the visitors went on to complete a 3-0 series win.

*

Allan Border took a reasonable dislike to the English, particularly members of the press:

"I am not talking to anyone in the British media. They are all pricks."

Compatriot Glenn McGrath was another who was always ready to get stuck into the Poms via the daily papers:

"When I say you'll lose the Ashes 3-0 I mean it as a compliment. Before every other series I reckoned we were going to beat you 5-0."

And the Aussie press in general were merciless during the 2001 Ashes campaign with questions like:

"What do you call an Englishman with a hundred runs against his name?"

"A bowler."

*

Of course sometimes the press themselves get stuck into you. The *Guardian* fired this broadside at Matthew Hayden in 2005 after the Australian batsman released a cookbook:

"The Matthew Hayden Cookbook is available from most bad bookshops."

*

England's Kevin Pietersen (Zola Budd to some sledgers and Fig jam to the rest – Fuck I'm good, just ask me) received a tremendous amount of stick from the country of his birth when he toured South Africa in 2005. He took revenge on the pitch with his bat but wasn't shy of using the media to have a crack at the opposition either. This was aimed at home captain Graeme Smith, who'd previously had spats with England captain Michael Vaughn, amongst others:

"He has no wit. I don't think he's too intelligent, actually. I know a lot of people who have no time for him, including his own players."

*

Former England captain Ray Illingworth offered his opinion on Ian Botham's captaincy:

"His idea of team spirit was to squirt a water pistol at someone and then go and get pissed."

And Botham couldn't let that pass without having a swipe back, this from 1995:

"If I had my way I would take him to the Traitor's Gate and hang, draw and quarter him."

*

Merv Hughes was a thorn in England's side throughout the 1980s but Martin Johnson described his 'mincing' run up as being like:

"Someone in high heels and a panty girdle chasing after a bus."

And you could always sledge the big man with:

"You run like a shopping trolley on a cobbled street."

4
THE DISMISSAL

Keen observers will note that Australian fast bowler Merv Hughes (also known as the fruitfly for his habit of annoying everyone during rain breaks) has more than his fair share of entries in this compilation. However, with such a rich crop to choose from, it's difficult to leave some of his best lines out. As with all dismissals, there is not a great deal the batsman can say as he trudges off to the pavilion, and Hughes was a master at sending them packing. The big Victorian was bowling at West Indian captain Viv Richards and after every delivery he stopped and stared at the 'master-blaster'. After several overs of this, Richards felt obliged to say something:

"This is my island, my culture. Don't you be staring at me. In my culture we just bowl."

Hughes, of course, knew he had his man, and bowled Richards shortly afterwards, dismissing him with:

"In my culture we just say 'fuck off'."

Richards, however, had his way more often than not. He was a supremely talented batsman who averaged over 50 in Test matches and had the rare ability to turn a game by destroying any bowling attack. Most cricket authorities

– players and commentators alike – agree that his regal air of invincibility at the crease was extremely unnerving for the bowler. He was already one up before facing the first delivery. Here he gets down on one knee and pleads with the umpire to let Leicestershire's Gordon Parsons bowl another bouncer in the over, the first having been smashed out of the ground:

"No, umpire, he can bowl as many of those as he wants."

This next quote is pure Richards, although it has been attributed to any number of batsmen since, such is its universal appeal. Glamorgan's Greg Thomas hurled down a wicked out-swinger that beat the Somerset legend all ends up. The pace-man quipped:

"It's red and round and weighs about five ounces. Can't you see it?"

There's nothing like teeing yourself up for a fall. Richards got hold of the next ball, smashing it into the river outside the ground. Seeing the stunned look on Thomas's face, he replied:

"You know what it looks like. Go get it!"

Many cricketers have been drawn into this one. It is said that the South African all-rounder Shaun Pollock beat Ricky Ponting's bat and immediately described the ball to him, only for Ponting to smash the next delivery for four with the same retort. This quip should not perhaps be in the dismissal section, but it qualifies on the grounds of being utterly dismissive.

*

More often than not there is no reply to the abuse once you've been given out. Australian wicketkeeper Ian Healy loved to fire a few parting shots at the batsman. This was aimed at Ben Hollioake, who thought he'd scored a pretty good half century:

"Now fuck off back to the nets, dickhead."

To which there aren't many meaningful replies. Aussie fast bowler Craig McDermott at least tried to redress the balance in favour of the departing batsman by loosing a broadside at Phil 'the cat' Tufnell after the Englishman had dismissed him in 1991:

"You've got to bat on this in a minute, Tuffers. Hospital food suit you?"

This might seem like a quip loaded with sour grapes but therein lies an even greater insult. For Tufnell to be batting 'in a minute' there would have to be a truly monumental collapse as Tufnell was rarely allowed to bat above the dizzy heights of number eleven. Ian Chappell also liked to have a quick dig at the England spinner:

"The other advantage England have got when Tufnell is

bowling is that he isn't fielding. "

But Ian Botham could always be relied upon to reply on behalf of the English:

"Chappell is a coward. He needs a crowd around him before he'll say anything. He's sour like milk that has been sitting in the sun for a week. "

Former captain Mike Brearley was equally dismissive of the Australian:

"Playing against a side captained by Chappell turns a cricket match into gang warfare. "

✻

Fred Trueman usually had a word or two with a dismissed batsman, occasionally delving into the sarcasm file. This was delivered to one of Oxford University's batsmen after he'd spent a good half minute inspecting and prodding the pitch before being castled by the Yorkshireman's first ball:

"Oh, bad luck, sir. And you were just getting settled in. "

✻

Words aren't always needed to give the batsman the send-off you think he deserves. Welsh Rugby captain

Gareth Thomas scored a try for the British Lions in New Zealand in 2005. He grounded the ball and then stood, patting both hands on the top of his head, a gesture known in the sporting world as the 'Ayatollah', as it copied the way Iranian nationals paid tribute to Khomeini. Shane Warne was disappointed to get out to Simon Jones at Trent Bridge in 2005 and utterly flabbergasted to be 'Ayatollahed' back to the pavilion. While the leg-spinner believed Jones thought him to be his rabbit, the press suggested the gesture was a dig at Warne's use of hair replacement products. The incident, whatever its intention, seems to have unsettled the Australian. Incidentally, former England captain Mike Brearley was known to Australian fans as The Ayatollah because of his beard.

*

In the 1996 World Cup quarter final between India and Pakistan, Pakistan's Aamer Sohail smashed a delivery from Venkatesh Prasad through a huge gap in the field for four runs. Seeing that no one was going to get the ball Sohail directed Prasad to the boundary with his bat to retrieve it himself. Of course you know what's going to happen next. Prasad bowled Sohail the following ball and simply directed the Pakistani batsman to the pavilion.

*

There are times when the batsman needs a word or two

in his ear to get him off the pitch. England's Simon Jones had left the field during the fourth Test at Trent Bridge in 2005 to have a scan on an injured ankle. Durham's Gary Pratt came on as a replacement fielder and proceeded to run out Australian captain Ricky Ponting just after tea on day three. Third umpire Mark Benson confirmed Aleem Dar's suspicion that Ponting was out and replayed the incident on the big screen. Ponting suddenly lost control and, in the words of Kevin Pietersen:

"he started effing and blinding at us"

Normally one of the more reserved players, England's Matthew Hoggard (a net bowler when compared with McGrath and Kasprowicz according to Jeff Thomson) stepped in to help Ponting make the right decision:

"I saw him having a go at Aleem Dar and as I went past him I told him he was out and that he'd better get off the field."

Ponting was upset that several times in the series England appeared to be resting their bowlers and bringing on substitute fielders, one of whom had just cost him his wicket, although whether there was a safe run available is debatable. In this case there can be no doubt that Jones was injured because he'd been taken to hospital. Andrew Flintoff recalls:

"Jones was off the field so we're not going to get the worst fielder to replace him, are we?"

Simon Jones added fuel to the fire by saying:

"Had I been on the field I would have run him out by yards anyway."

As Ponting left the field he looked up at the English balcony and launched a blistering verbal assault on coach Duncan Fletcher. Fletcher dismissed the incident with:

"I smiled at Ricky but he didn't smile back. He was in a terrible temper for some reason though quite why he was blaming me when his partner, Damien Martyn, had called him for a suicidal single I don't know. I heard him mumble something but I didn't hear exactly what he said. All the palaver made me burn my toast."

*

The crowds aren't too shy about letting the batsman know what they thought about the way he got out either. Ian Botham made a pair in the second Test at Lord's in the Ashes contest in 1981, his twelfth as captain. As he trudged back to the pavilion there wasn't a single ripple of applause from the crowd, not a murmur throughout the ground. He famously resigned the captaincy soon thereafter and then, with the freedom of a player released from those shackles, dominated the rest of a series that became known as 'Botham's Ashes'. Geraint Jones, England's wicketkeeper for the 2005 Ashes battle, recalls a different reaction. He'd just danced down the track to Shane Warne, not the wisest course of action against the magician, and then sliced the shot straight to Kasprowicz. The crowd let him know how they felt with:

"What did you think you were doing? Don't you know that he's the best bowler in the world?"

Jones, who'd been born in Papua New Guinea, reportedly left Australia as a young man because he was fed up with being called Grant. There were other ways of sledging him, however:

"You wouldn't get in Queensland seconds."

"As a wicketkeeper-batsman, you're George Lazenby to Gilchrist's Connery."

Team-mate Kevin Pietersen had to endure far more than the occasional comment when he toured South Africa in 2005, this line relating to his unusual haircut:

"Get that dead mongoose off your head."

The rest of the squad remember the crowds giving him bucketfuls of abuse but the cavalier batsman silenced them with a series of blistering one-day knocks that would eventually be enough to oust stalwart Graham Thorpe from the Test line-up for the coming Ashes series.

England's Allan Lamb was another who was targeted

because of his South African accent. Fast bowler Allan Donald had sent down a couple of quick bouncers, which Lamb had managed to avoid but he couldn't get any bat on them. Donald quipped:

"Lambie, if you want to drive, go hire a car."

Lamb cover drove the next ball beautifully for four and replied:

"Go park that fucker!"

*

South Africa ran into more trouble at the Oval in 1994. England's Devon Malcolm, never one to look like troubling the scorers with bat in hand, had been hit on the head by a delivery from Fanie de Villiers when he remarked:

"You guys are history."

When his radar was working there was no doubt that Malcolm was one of the most hostile bowlers ever to play the game, and the knock on the helmet certainly fired him up. He ripped through the South African batting line-up to finish the innings with figures of nine for 57 after an incredible spell of pace bowling.

*

England's Darren Gough removed Aussie batsman Shane Watson in a one-day NatWest match in 2005 and promptly ran round him shrieking and waving his arms like a ghost. This was a wonderful non-verbal sledge about the fact that Watson had become so spooked on a tour of Lumley Castle in Chester-le-Street that he had spent the night sleeping on Brett Lee's hotel room floor. For the rest of the series the English crowds cheered him to the wicket with the theme tune from the film *Ghostbusters*. To add further insult to the batsman, Gough also sledged him with:

"You can sleep on my floor tonight."

*

Just to show that the dismissal has been used for a while longer than the thirty or so years reported so far, here's a nice reply from Yorkshire's bowler Emmott Robinson having just delivered a cracker to Surrey's Smyth-Foulkes in 1936. The southerner initiated the action with:

"Well bowled, sir, that was a wonderful delivery."

"Aye, and it were bloody wasted on thee."

*

It should be mentioned that sometimes the dismissing sledge doesn't work, to the general disbelief of the fielding side. In a Test match against India in Mumbai in

2001, Australian Michael Slater appeared to have caught Rahul Dravid after the latter had mistimed a pull shot. Slater celebrated, but neither the umpire or batsman were convinced that the catch had been taken cleanly and Dravid stood his ground. Slater was incensed and subjected both men to a barrage of abuse, even though the replays showed it was unlikely that he'd taken the catch. Dravid was embroiled in another firestorm when he swatted South African fast bowler Allan Donald for ten runs in two balls during a one-day final in 1997. Donald marched up to him and shouted:

"This isn't such a fucking easy game."

Dravid took exception to the comment and accused Donald of using racially inappropriate language, a fact that the South African strenuously denied. He used similar words, though, in a magnificent sporting duel with England's Mike Atherton at Trent Bridge in 1998. England needed to resist the 'quick' chasing 247 to win the match. Atherton was thoroughly worked over by a barrage of Donald bouncers and verbal abuse, including staying put after a caught behind appeal led Donald to shout:

"You're a fucking cheat!"

England held on with Atherton and Alec Stewart (Alan Partridge) guiding them home by eight wickets. Australian wicketkeeper Ian Healy sledged Atherton with the same line during the third Ashes Test of the

1990-91 tour. Healy believed Atherton had edged the ball and shouted the above line at the batsman. Atherton, refusing to walk, simply turned to the 'keeper and said:

"When in Rome."

England's summer 2011 home series against the all-conquering Indians was expected to be a close and hard-fought encounter but the tourists lost key bowler Zaheer Khan to injury in the first Test and England thrashed them 4-0 to claim the top spot on the Test rankings table. With England racking up the runs at the Oval in the fourth Test, Sreesanth and night-watchman Jimmy Anderson got stuck into a battle of wits. Sreesanth repeatedly sledged Anderson for playing and missing, and Anderson returned fire having cracked the Indian's bowling to the boundary. Sreesanth then decided to give up on the verbals and simply stare Anderson down after every ball. Anderson eventually nicked one to VVS Laxman in the slip cordon and Sreesanth sent him on his way with another prolonged stare, which has since been labelled the greatest silent sledge. In the commentary box, former England player David Lloyd delighted in the confrontation:

"I think it's a great stare. I love it. It must be so frustrating for them because they're big, strapping chaps but it's a non-contact sport so you can't tackle, you can't kick, and you can't punch. So you can just stare and have a little word here and there."

THE VIEW IN ASIA

With the spread of the Commonwealth in the eighteenth and nineteenth centuries, the game of cricket was taken from the green fields of England to the farthest corners of the earth. The four main cricket-playing nations on the sub-continent – India, Pakistan, Sri Lanka and Bangladesh – were introduced to the game by British explorers during this period of English imperial conquest. In keeping with the traditions of fair play, these countries adopted the game and the spirit in which it was played. The peoples of southern Asia already existed in communities where being polite and keeping face were part of the fabric of society. When it arrived from Australasia, sledging on the pitch was alien to them, and was seen as being employed by base and uneducated players. As a result, Asian cricketers didn't quite know how to deal with the abuse, although they toughened up pretty quickly. By 2000 India's Sourav Ganguly was known to the Australian media as the 'bad boy of international cricket', with his armoury of tasteless sledges unnerving the Aussie batsmen. It is also possible for the Asian teams to avoid punishment from the umpires when they're abroad because they can sledge opponents with the most foul language as long as it's concealed by a local tongue that can't be understood by the officials. However, sometimes even the umpires feel they have to interrupt play to give the fielding captain some abuse, in the clearest English no less. The most famous incident occurred when England captain Mike Gatting moved a fielder behind the batsman in

Faisalabad in 1987. He denied there was any intention of concealing the movement from the batsman but umpire Shakoor Rana stormed up to Gatting and called him a:

"Fucking cheating cunt"

Gatting is said to have told Rana exactly the same thing and the match had to be suspended pending a full written apology from Gatting, which he then penned under considerable duress.

5
MORE SHARP
PRACTICES

Sledging is only one of a long list of underhand practices
employed by fielding teams to remove opposing batsmen.
W.G. Grace's indiscretions are well documented, and
some have been listed earlier, but would the great man
have ever resorted to scuffing the pitch on a good length
to help his bowlers, tampering with the ball, claiming
it hadn't crossed the boundary rope, or appealing for a
catch after the ball had bounced? The batsmen are not
immune either. How many decide not to walk when they
know they've edged the ball to the wicketkeeper but the
umpire hasn't heard the nick?

OVER-APPEALING

In May 2006, Nottinghamshire and England wicketkeeper
Chris Read became increasingly irate with Sussex spinner
Mushtaq Ahmed after the bowler repeatedly appealed
for dubious LBW decisions. Read was eventually given
out but he confronted the spinner, an incident for which
he apologised later. The practice of over-appealing in
the hope that the umpire will eventually buckle to the
pressure is not new. Indeed many players have been
warned that their persistent appealing and running to the

umpires contravenes the spirit of the game, most notably the English teams of the 1880s and the Australians under Ricky Ponting in the last few years. Justin Langer claims that the very nature of the game can lead to a particularly vociferous appeal after a prolonged period of high tension or drama:

"Over-appealing is almost the nature of the game in those circumstances."

The ICC tried to stamp it out during a meeting of the various boards in Malaysia in 2001 but six Indian players were censured two months later for breaching this code of conduct. The practice does look set to die out now that the review system is in place, however. Both teams are given the opportunity to review the umpire's decision on LBWs and contentious catches. This should ensure that the right decision is made.

It must be said that the fielder usually knows whether the catch has been taken, but there are occasions, such as when a player dives forward at slip to take a low chance, when they might have their eyes closed and may not feel the bounce immediately before gathering the ball, but this is rare. It became commonplace for Australian players to appeal for anything close to a catch in the 1980s and '90s but this has been addressed with the introduction of the review system, although when the TV evidence is inconclusive Ricky Ponting still believes the fielder's word should be taken.

BALL TAMPERING

Ball tampering is the illegal modification of the ball by a player so that it behaves differently, either through the air or after it has pitched. If its behaviour can be altered, the batsmen may not play it as well and they're more likely to get out. It is not as common now – the grounds being saturated with close-up television cameras that can pick the culprit out – but it was often used by the fielding side to make a breakthrough as recently as 2000. The methods most commonly employed are: to pick or lift the stitched seam; to rub the ball on the ground; to rub any substance into the ball's surface other than saliva or sweat; to scar the ball with nails or studs.

Pakistan pace-man Waqar Younis was given a one-match suspension following ball tampering allegations on a tour of England in 1992. He and fellow bowler Wasim Akram dominated the English batsmen with their reverse swing and went on to win the series 2-1. Team mate Shoaib Akhtar was also investigated during the 1999 World Cup but no action was taken.

England's Michael Atherton was picked up by the television cameras at Lord's in 1994 appearing to rub dirt into the ball to roughen one side up in order to make it swing. His team were having problems dismissing the South African batsmen and he, somewhat foolishly, resorted to this underhand tactic, for which he was fined £2000 and almost lost the captaincy. The *Daily Mirror* chipped in with the headline: The Soiled Skipper. While commentating with Ian Botham in 2006, the great all-rounder reminded the opener of the incident.

Botham: *"They've thrown the ball to Trescothick. Did they ever let you shine the ball, Athers?"*

Atherton (chuckles): *"Sometimes."*

Botham: *"And what did you use to polish it?"*

Atherton: *"Saliva normally."*

Botham: *"And on the other occasions? A trowel? Gardening gloves?"*

Atherton: *"Boiled sweets were actually quite good."*

Botham: *"Oh, that's what it was."*

SCUFFING THE PITCH

Umpires try to protect the pitch so that the bowler's footmarks do not cause the batsmen any problems with uneven bounce, which could be dangerous. An imaginary strip five feet from the popping crease, two feet wide and the length of the pitch is carefully watched by the umpires to make sure that the bowlers do not encroach and scuff the pitch on a good line and length. If a bowler does follow through into this area, he will be warned by the umpire. Repeated warnings may mean the exclusion of the player from the attacking line-up.

This doesn't mean, of course, that some players won't deliberately try to scuff the pitch in order to give their bowlers something to aim at. Shane Warne is a master of exploiting the footmarks at the batsman's end, arcing the ball into this rough to get greater purchase on his devilish leg-spinners. If his side can increase the size of the footmarks, then so much the better.

The best-known case of a fielder deliberately scuffing the pitch on a length concerns Pakistan's all-rounder Shahid Afridi in a 2005 encounter with England in Faisalabad. The match had been halted while police investigated a gas explosion outside the ground when, with everyone's attention diverted, Afridi marched across and pirouetted on the pitch, his studs breaking up the surface. England's Marcus Trescothick pointed out the marks to the umpires and television replays confirmed the action. Afridi was banned for a Test and two one-day internationals.

MATCH FIXING

The most famous case of a player attempting to influence the outcome of matches concerns the then South African captain Hansie Cronje, when, in 2000, he admitted to providing bookmakers with information on pitch conditions, weather reports, team selection and likely declaration totals. He'd been trapped after phone taps installed by Delhi police had recorded him apparently talking with an Indian bookie. However, there were more serious charges to be laid at his door. It seemed he had taken money to influence the outcome of some games, offering Herschelle Gibbs and seamer Henry Williams cash to alter the result of a one-day international in India. Neither player fulfilled his supposed part in the scam, but they were still banned for six months. Cronje was banned for life by the King Commission. Sadly there is no happy ending to the saga. Cronje was killed in a plane crash in 2002. He was, however, involved in one of the game's great sledges. He'd been demolishing the bowling of Merv Hughes while the Australians were on tour in the early '90s and Merv was getting pretty fed up. Having watched the ball sail over the boundary rope yet again, he headed down to Cronje, let out a massive fart, and said:

"Try hitting that for six."

Although the Cronje case was the highest profile incidence of a player trying to affect the outcome of a match, others have been tempted to offer the bookies information on selections and match reports in return for financial incentives.

Indians Ajay Jadeja, Manoj Prabhakar, Ajay Sharma, Mohammed Azharuddin and physiotherapist Ali Irani were all banned for their roles in match fixing scams, Jadeja being forced to serve a five-year ban from 2000. Indian Salim Malik and Pakistan's Ata-ur Rehman received life bans at the same time. England's Alec Stewart was embroiled in another incident when Indian bookie M.K. Gupta claimed to have paid the former captain £5,000 for inside information in 2000, an allegation that the Surrey man strenuously denied. Kiwi Martin Crowe was named by the same bookie in 1992, and although Crowe admitted accepting £2,000 for what he thought were interviews for an article, he later broke off contact having realised that Gupta was a bookmaker. Gupta himself claimed to have paid out £14,000 for the supposed interview, and also named Aussie Mark Waugh, West Indian captain Brian Lara, and Sri Lankan pair Arjuna Ranatunga and Aravinda de Silva in his defence. Hopefully the incidences of match fixing will decline now that the ICC has set up an Anti Corruption and Security Unit (ACSU), although anti-corruption investigations carried out by the former police chief Sir Paul Condon indicate it is still happening.

Indeed, just when cricket thought it had cleaned itself up, three Pakistani players (Mohammad Amir, Mohammad Asif and captain Salman Butt) were banned for spot-fixing (bowling deliberate no-balls at certain points in the match) during their 2010 tour of England in an attempt to defraud bookmakers.

REFUSING TO WALK

This issue has cropped up again recently with Australian captain Ricky Ponting calling for a game-wide agreement on appealing for catches. This came in the wake of Matthew Hayden claiming a catch at first slip off South African batsman Jacques Rudolph. The latter refused to walk, believing the ball to have dropped short of the fieldsman. The television replay was inconclusive and the umpires decided to give Rudolph his marching orders based on their reading of the situation. It's difficult to blame Rudolph in this incidence as no batsman is likely to walk if he thinks there is some doubt over the catch, and with the umpires now being able to use replays it seemed sensible to wait for the decision from the third umpire.

An area of contention lies in the number of caught behinds that occur off faint edges. The fielders may know instinctively that the ball has been touched, but the umpire may not, and may return a verdict of 'not out'. Some batsmen will not walk simply because they have not been given out, others will walk even though the umpire would not have given the decision against them. It's a contentious issue, and one that cannot be resolved by Ponting's call for all claimed catches to stand. Thankfully the review system, which will soon include both snicko and hotspot, should make the vast majority of umpiring decisions correct, but when a team has used its reviews some errors may still occur. In the 2010-11 Sydney Ashes Test Ian Bell was given out caught behind but he refused to walk. Although he was roundly booed by the crowd the hotspot replay proved he hadn't hit the ball and he went on to make a crucial century.

What the game really needs is honesty, particularly when the umpires aren't able to make the right call. Honesty was the last thing on the Australian team's minds when they appealed for a close catch in the same Ashes Test in Sydney. Alistair Cook was on 99 when he clipped the ball to Phil Hughes at short leg. Hughes and Haddin didn't look convinced that the ball had carried but when the rest of the team went up they joined in the raucous appeal. Thankfully the umpires referred the decision to the third umpire. Slow motion replays clearly showed the ball bouncing well short of the fielder, prompting commentator Ian Botham to say:

"That's absolutely dreadful. In fact it's cheating."

What would injured captain Ricky Ponting have thought? England had the last laugh, however. Cook smashed a magnificent 189 and England won the match by an innings, securing the Ashes with a comfortable 3-1 series win.

South Africa will rue the fact that the review system wasn't in place during their 2010-11 home series against India. With the tourists chasing 340 to win at Newlands, spinner Paul Harris floated a beautiful delivery onto Rahul Dravid's pads. Although the ball clipped the bat immediately afterwards, the umpire couldn't be sure of the LBW and gave Dravid another life. If South Africa had been allowed to review the decision, they would have seen the ball hitting middle stump and the decision would have been reversed. It is these 'howlers', as Nasser Hussain calls them, that the review system is designed to eradicate. Of course Dravid could have done a Kevin Pietersen and walked after an LBW was turned down but India were desperate to get something out of the series and he stood his ground.

*

In the 1946-47 series England captain Wally Hammond loudly chirped this line to Don Bradman after the Australian had refused to walk during the first Test in Brisbane:

"That's a fine fucking way to start a series."

Adam Gilchrist let India's Mohammed Kaif (Tendulkar's bag carrier according to Nasser Hussain) know his stance on such matters having appeared to take a fair catch behind the stumps:

"That was off your glove and the whole world's watching. At least we know you're not a walker."

Ian Botham countered on the Indian's behalf with:

"If you're playing Australia you don't walk."

South Africa's legendary batsman Barry Richards agreed:

"The only time an Australian walks is when his car runs out of petrol."

And this Malcolm Marshall line was delivered to Steve Waugh after he refused to walk in the early 1980s:

"You convicts are all the same. Are your legs still chained

together?"

Surely the most bizarre incidence of not walking occurred in the fifth one-day international at Jamshedpur, India, in April 2006. India were in some trouble against England when the tourists threw the ball to part-time off-break bowler Kevin Pietersen. He lobbed one up at Harbhajan Singh, the ball gripped in the rough, turned and flicked the top of the Indian's off stump. He was flabbergasted. Pietersen is one of the most destructive batsmen in world cricket, but he's not known as a bowler and Singh was adamant that the ball couldn't have cleaned him up. He had to be given out by the umpire before he would walk, and this having just been clean bowled! Pietersen, of course, couldn't resist firing a quick sledge at the departing batsman:

"I told you I was an all-rounder."

Ricky Ponting was once again the centre of attention in the 2010-11 home Ashes series against the old enemy. Even after the umpires had reviewed a caught behind appeal during the fourth Test at the MCG, and correctly found Kevin Pietersen not out (his bat had brushed his pad, with neither anywhere near the ball), Ponting argued for over a minute with on-field umpires Aleem Dar and Tony Hill. It's difficult to explain his conduct given that the incident was replayed on the big screen, with the third umpire's verdict clearly vindicated. For his outburst, Ponting was fined 40% of his match fee, but that didn't stop him confronting Pietersen when he'd finished with the umpires. England went on to win the match comfortably and retain the Ashes.

*

Whatever your view on sledging it has become an integral part of the game. Whether it should be restricted to the casual comment about someone's ability, or brandished as a potent weapon remains open to debate, but there's no doubt that some of cricket's finest moments have come about as a direct result of a good sledge or lightning reply. The author prefers not to take things to extremes but is quite happy to offer the batsmen his opinion on the occasional Sunday that he does play. This was delivered to the two men at the crease in the Hollybush Tavern versus Capel match in 2005:

"Just stop the boundaries, lads. These two have eaten far too much at tea to be able to run between the wickets."

He might also offer a welcome of sorts:

"Oh dear, someone get the tennis ball from the car."

Or the sledge after the batsman has played and missed:

"What are you going to do when I'm warmed up and bowling at 30 mph?"

"I've seen better swinging in a nightclub."

"You couldn't hit water if you fell off a boat."

"When I left this morning your girlfriend told me that you'd been off your stroke in the bedroom too."

Or the chirp to the umpire when the batsman has been given not out:

"How do you spell LBW?"

And the dismissal:

"Don't worry, I didn't see it either."

The important thing to note here is that the banter is not threatening or abusive but it might help to unsettle the batsman and bring about a wicket, which is the intention. These lines can be supplemented with:

"Whatever we do, we can't afford to get this guy out. The next one might be able to play."

If the batsman gets an obvious nick but the umpire turns down the appeal, one of the fielders should chip in with:

"Pass me the ball. I've got some tweezers to pull the splinters out."

"Your bat is like a doughnut: all edge and no middle."

✴

We are constantly reminded of the goodness that underlies cricket when we compare it with other sports, football in particular. Think of the moment Andrew Flintoff consoled a beaten but defiant Brett Lee (Tin Tin) after the nail-biting finish in the 2005 Edgbaston Test, or the way Lee returned the sentiment at Old Trafford when England, try as they might, could not take the last wicket and Australia held on for an important draw. Both images stay in the mind long after the events themselves and were rightly considered the finest sporting gestures of the year. Faith in the game has been restored. Although it should be mentioned that when Flintoff crouched to shake Lee's hand, he apparently whispered:

"That's one-one, you bastard!"

Another example of fine sportsmanship was needed to calm a volatile situation in the 2011 England – India Test match at Trent Bridge. England were scoring freely through Ian Bell and Eoin Morgan, with the former on 137, when Morgan clipped the ball down to long leg off the last delivery before tea. Praveen Kumar made a brave attempt to stop the ball going for four but it bounced off his leg and ran alongside the boundary rope. He couldn't see where it had gone so the batsmen assumed it had hit the rope. Bell promptly left his crease and joined Morgan before they both trotted off for a well-earned break. But the umpires suspected the ball hadn't hit the rope and didn't signal that the over had been bowled and that it was indeed teatime. Kumar threw the ball in to Indian captain MS Dhoni and he passed it to Abhinav

Mukund, who then flicked off the bails and appealed for a run out. The umpires called the departing batsmen back and asked to be shown the television replay. When the replay revealed that the ball was still live and that Bell had simply assumed it was tea, the umpires asked Dhoni if he wished to uphold his appeal. He did, and Bell was given out. The crowd reacted angrily and both the Indian players and umpires were roundly booed from the field. During the tea interval, England captain Andrew Strauss and coach Andy Flower asked Dhoni to reconsider and withdraw his appeal. Dhoni had already discussed it with his team and, to his credit, agreed. The incident didn't sit well with him or his players and they made the collective decision to ask Bell to bat again. It is interesting to note that most former players agreed that they would have appealed and, without having the tea interval to consider the event more carefully, would not have withdrawn it. Although Bell appears to have made an honest mistake, he acted carelessly (batting partner Eoin Morgan was aware that the ball was live because he grounded his bat in his crease and appeared to try to tell Bell to get back to his). When the Indian players returned to the arena after tea, the crowd was even more hostile, but the jeers turned to cheers when Bell joined them on the pitch. Indeed only Bell emerges from the incident in the red for his moment of doziness. The umpires stuck to the letter of the law and asked Dhoni what he wished to do, and the Indian captain ensured the game went ahead in the right spirit.

*

Jim Maxwell offered his opinion after that incredible 2005 Ashes series, in which both teams went at it hammer and tongs on the field but were prepared to chew over the day's play with a beer afterwards:

"Comparing the conduct and behaviour of cricketers and footballers has won respect for cricket, as football opens its doors to more of the same histrionics that demean the integrity of the game. Yes, sledging can be distasteful and unnecessary, though it's occasionally leavened by subtlety or humour."

He offers more on the respect for the officials by the players:

"One of the outstanding virtues of cricket is the acceptance of the umpire's decision."

Just ask yourself when was the last time you saw a footballer agree with a referee's correct decision, let alone the times when they get it wrong? Now think of a poor umpiring decision when the batsman has been given out LBW having clearly edged the ball first. It is extremely rare for there to be any reaction other than mild surprise from the batsman as he trudges back to the pavilion. It must be said that the good and bad decisions in both sports probably even themselves out, but that is not the perception having watched them for a number of years.

Fans and players alike know instinctively what is and

what isn't acceptable behaviour. Most appreciate the odd sharp glance or chirp, and it's both rewarding and enjoyable when the batsman fires a comment back. Where the practice becomes unacceptable is when the fielding side lose their tempers and their ability to remain in control. This can lead to tirades of personal abuse and aggressive swearing, and most would agree that the line between fair play and improper conduct has been breached.

6
BEST OF THE REST

SOME OF THE FINEST SLEDGES FROM THE WORLD OF SPORT

Don't believe for a moment that sledging is confined to the green ovals of the world. Although the practice became popularised by cricket, it is not uncommon to hear of a worthy sledge from any number of sports. Here are some of the more notable spats from around the sporting world.

SNOOKER

You wouldn't think that the game of snooker could almost bring opponents to blows but Australian Quentin Hann and England's Andy Hicks came out fighting after their first round encounter at the Crucible in the 2004 Embassy World Championship in Sheffield. The two had exchanged words before shaking hands as Hicks completed a 10-4 victory. Hann had said how much he'd enjoyed beating Hicks on their three previous encounters, to which the Englishman replied:

"Well at least I'm still in the top sixteen."

Hann appeared to lose his temper and brandish his cue at

this point, replying:

*"You're short, bald, and always will be, and you can
have me outside whenever you want."*

The match referee intervened at this point. Hann
apologised for his behaviour afterwards but still made
this offer, for the sum of £50,000 no less:

*"Let's get it on. Even if it wasn't for money it would still
be interesting to face Andy in the ring."*

The game's greatest natural player is also not one to shy
away from a controversial situation. During his 2005
quarter-final match with Peter Ebdon, Ronnie O'Sullivan
became so impatient at Ebdon's slow play that he asked
a spectator what time it was. The Essex Exocet became
even more irate when Ebdon took three minutes over a
single shot and five minutes to make a break of twelve,
and then insisted on having the cue ball cleaned every
few shots. O'Sullivan began laughing at this point,
tried to play with a towel over his head, made faces at
the cameras and behind Ebdon's back, and continued
playing even when he needed ten snookers to win the
frame. Ebdon's tactics worked, however, and he went on
to win 13-11.

Footballer Jason McAteer apparently met Jimmy White
in Dublin and greeted him with the wholly inappropriate
welcome:

"One hundred and eighty!"

And Alex Higgins reportedly introduced himself to Stephen Hendry before their match with:

"Hello. I'm the Devil."

TENNIS

You couldn't write a book about verbal abuse without including a line or two from the grandmaster of the practice. Enter John McEnroe, or Superbrat as he has been called on occasion. Tennis is considered to be a beautiful game of skill, guile and power but McEnroe brought a rough edge to his brilliance on the court. He was ultra-competitive and claimed that his rants, although not apparently designed to put off an opponent unless the abuse was aimed directly at them, allowed him to up his game. Let's enjoy a few of his finer moments, firstly, with a volley or two at the officials:

"Man, you cannot be serious!"

"You can't see as well as these fucking flowers, and they're fucking plastic."

"You're a disgrace to mankind."

And now to the spectators:

"I'm so disgusting that you shouldn't watch. Everybody,

The Sledger's Handbook

leave!"

"You got a fucking appointment to get to, asshole?"

"What other problems do you have besides being unemployed, a moron and a dork?"

These two comments were saved for opponent Brad Gilbert during an end-change in the Masters Cup in 1986:

"You don't deserve to be on the same court as me."

"You are the worst, the fucking worst!"

But Mac saved this for himself, quoted from an interview with the *Independent* in 2005:

"I remember a poll in a Miami paper to find the worst people of all time. Charles Manson was one, Attila the Hun was two, I was three and Jack the Ripper was four."

Romanian nasty boy Ilie Nastase was another who enjoyed baiting the opposition. Here's a line delivered to Gene Meyer in a veterans' event in 2005:

"Ace me and I'll pull my pants down."

Meyer did. Nastase did.

FOOTBALL

There was always going to be a section on football given the amount of bad language and abuse that permeates the game. The first of these is a fine comment delivered by referee Tom Wharton to volatile and dentally challenged Hearts winger John Hamilton in the 1960s, as quoted by the *Independent*. Wharton sent Hamilton from the field, dismissing him with the words:

"The time has come, Mr Hamilton, for you to rejoin your teeth."

*

In the 1990s, and with the arrival of the premier league, old footballing rivalries resurfaced. The seeds of discontent had been sown between Manchester United and Arsenal in an FA Cup match at Highbury in 1987, however. United's Brian McClair missed a penalty, which prompted Arsenal's Nigel Winterburn to observe:

"You're shit, you are."

McClair bided his time, waiting for the right moment to take revenge, but it wasn't until the 1990-91 season that he got his chance. Winterburn had gone down under a heavy challenge and McClair stepped up behind him and repeatedly kicked him in the back. Anders Limpar retaliated for the hosts which sparked an all-in brawl. Both sides were eventually docked points under the league's new disciplinary system. Their rivalry continues to this day, with repeated confrontations between players and managers on and off the field, including the now notorious (though alleged) 'pizza gate' fast-food throwing incident between Arsène Wenger and Alex Ferguson in the Old Trafford tunnel in 2003.

Manchester United's Roy Keane was always going to be a likely contributor in this section and he doesn't let us down with this comment to Patrick Vieira – who does a lot of charity work in the land of his birth – in the tunnel at Highbury in 2005 (reported by Mike Walker in the *Guardian*):

"If you love Senegal so much, why don't you play for them?"

Vieira apparently didn't reply immediately but chose his rebuke having considered Keane's acrimonious departure from his international team in 2002:

"For someone who leaves his team at the World Cup, he should keep this kind of remark to himself."

Keane had been sent home from the Far East after a bust up with Irish manager Mick McCarthy. He is reported to have told his boss:

"I don't rate you as a manager and I don't rate you as a person. Stick it up your bollocks, you English cunt."

*

And here's a classic crowd sledge, aimed at Rangers' goalkeeper Andy Goram after he'd been diagnosed with mild schizophrenia:

"There's only two Andy Gorams, two Andy Gorams…."

*

Of course the referees like to get involved, too. Here David Elleray explains why he's showing the yellow card to Birmingham City's antipodean winger Stan Lazaridis:

"Because you're Australian and you always beat us at everything."

And so do the commentary team, this backhander from Darragh Maloney:

"Scholes has four players in front of him, five if you count Gary Neville."

As do the managers. Here Ron Atkinson extols the virtues of underused England midfielder, Carlton Palmer:

"He can trap the ball further than I can kick it."

Even Gareth Southgate's mum had a word or two for her son after his penalty miss condemned England to defeat against the Germans at Wembley in the semi-final of Euro '96:

"Why didn't you just belt it?"

But we'll leave the last word on football to a man who was on the receiving end of the insults more often than not. Here Paul Gascoigne replies to the question of whether or not he has a message for the people of Norway:

"Yes. Fuck off."

BOXING

Let's now dive into the murky world of pugilism. As American Bernard Hopkins squared up to England's Howard Eastman, he told the challenger (according to the *Sun*):

"You should be scared. You're looking at one hell of a mean motherfucker."

*

And it wouldn't be right to overlook the self-proclaimed 'greatest of all time'. Before their 1974 'Rumble in the Jungle' clash, Muhammad Ali had promised George Foreman:

"I'm going to beat your Christian ass, you white flag-waving son-of-a-bitch."

During the fight itself, George Foreman had thrown everything he had, including the kitchen sink, at Muhammad Ali for eight energy-sapping rounds. He'd destroyed every other opponent he'd faced but had yet to finish Ali and was rapidly running out of steam. During a clinch Ali grabbed his head and shouted in his ear:

"Is that all you got, George? Is that it?"

Foreman admitted later that he was spent. He couldn't believe the amount of punishment Ali had taken, and was powerless to resist when Ali fought back off the ropes and won the fight towards the end of the eighth round.

*

And Mike Tyson could usually be relied upon for something nice to say about an opponent. He'd already been fined $335,000 for biting Lennox Lewis in the leg during one of the press conferences (he probably couldn't reach his ears) before he cranked up the tension in the build up to his 2002 fight with England's heavyweight champion in Memphis:

"Lennox Lewis, I'm coming for you, man. My style is impetuous, my defence is impregnable and I'm just ferocious. I want your heart. I want to eat his children."

Lewis gave the self-styled 'baddest man on the planet' a boxing lesson, finally ending Tyson's hopes in the eighth round of a one-sided contest.

RUGBY

The oval ball game, too, has its fair share of loudmouths, not least David Campese, the record-breaking Australian winger (or should that be whinger?), who constantly fuelled the fires of discontent between his side and the English. He was always bemoaning the fact the northern hemisphere teams couldn't compete with the best from 'down under' and even vowed to march down Oxford Street with a placard proclaiming England as the best side in the world if they won the 2003 World Cup, which they duly did. Thankfully, 'Campo' kept his word, although he did brand the team boring immediately afterwards. The New Zealand press weren't shy of getting stuck into the English either. Before their June 2003 clash in Wellington, the English pack were likened to 'a bunch of white orcs on steroids', a reference to the huge, ugly beasts from Peter Jackson's *The Lord of the Rings*. But the personal abuse between players is always worth a line or two. Let's enjoy Australian referee Peter Marshall's comment to Neil Back before ordering him to the blood bin in their November 2003 match against South Africa in Perth:

"Get off. You look ugly."

And here's a couple from the crowd trouble file, taken from a banner in the England-Australia World Cup Final match in Sydney later in the same tournament:

"If you want to XXXX the Aussies, use a Jonny."

England's fly-half Charlie Hodgson admitted that the Wallabies had got to him with a series of sledges in their 2004 clash at Twickenham, which the Aussies won 21-19, the standard line appearing to be:

"You can't kick."

Proof also that you can sledge your own team comes from England scrum-half Steve Smith to captain Bill Beaumont during Erica Roe's famous Twickenham streak in 1982:

"Hey, Bill, there's a bird coming on with your bum on her chest."

*

Legendary All Black hooker Sean Fitzpatrick packed down opposite Australian new boy Phil Kearns in 1989. Sensing Kearns was uncomfortable the Kiwi quipped:

"What are you doing here? You don't belong here. You're just a little boy. Why don't you go home to mummy?"

The rugby league boys, too, enjoy the odd moment of verbal jousting. Balmain prop George Piper was given instructions to bring down St George forward Kevin Ryan at all costs in their 1960 clash. He waited for the right moment then hit Ryan with a punch that would have:

"Ripped the head off a bullock."

Ryan shook off the blow, faced Piper and said:

Not a bad shot, George. Now you'll have to wait for yours."

Piper got himself sent off shortly afterwards. Some would say that was a pretty good decision.

England prop Phil Vickery was taking a good deal of abuse from the Australians in the 2003 Rugby World Cup final. Opposite number Bill Young was ribbing him about his size and weight, his lack of pace and his heart for the contest, but the 'Raging Bull' soon tired of the verbal jousting and shut Young up (and caused the rest of the Australian pack to have a quiet chuckle) with:

"If I knew who you were, I'd give you some banter back, but I don't."

In the semi-final against the mighty All Blacks, Australian captain George Gregan had also been on the receiving end of a number of tasteless Kiwi broadsides but his team rallied and caused the upset. Gregan, of course, had to get the last word in at the bottom of one ruck towards the end of the match:

"Four more years, boys. You're going to have to wait four more years!"

*

According to the *Guardian* when former Wales coach Graham Henry – then preparing the All Blacks for the Lions' visit – was asked whether senior player Gareth Thomas would make a good captain he replied:

"The short answer is 'no' and the longer answer is also 'no'."

Thomas went on to captain the Welsh to the 2005 Six Nations Grand Slam.

In his formative years as a rugby upstart, Brian Moore was getting a good helping of abuse from the Gloucester crowd so, at the next lineout, he turned and shouted to the stand:

"It's amazing how much noise 3000 people can make clapping with 7000 hands."

And after a particularly bruising Roundhay vs Headingley match, in which the young Moore had slugged it out with the opposition for the entire eighty minutes, an old committee member approached him and muttered:

"As long as I live, you'll never make it as a rugby player."

Moore is said to have replied:

"Why don't you fuck off? By the time I'm eligible to play senior rugby, you'll be dead anyway."

There's nothing like proving someone wrong, especially after they've aimed a sharply barbed sledge in your direction.

*****

I consulted a number of sources while
writing this book. They are listed below.

www.bbc.co.uk
www.forum.frankblack.net
www.cricket.mailliw.com
www.smh.com.au
www.theage.com.au
www.nobok.co.uk
www.content-usa.cricinfo.com
www.hinduonnet.com
www.telegraph.co.uk
www.en.wikipedia.org
www.abhishekmathur.blogspot.com
www.salixcc.com
www.paktribune.com
www.telegraph.co.uk/sport
www.guardian.co.uk/sport
www.cricinfo.com
www.espn.go.com

ESPN's Sporting duels
Sky TV's Football Years
BBC Television
Channel 9 Australian Television
The Big Book of Sporting Insults, David Milsted
The Fast Men, David Frith
The Big Book of More Sporting Insults, Jonathan L'Estrange
A Century of Great Cricket Quotes, David Hopps
Playing with Fire, Nasser Hussain
Serious, John McEnroe